contemporary guide

understanding

prints : a contemporary guide

Pat Gilmour

Waddington Galleries

Dimensions given are paper sizes unless otherwise stated.
Height is given before width.
The enlarged details facing the full page illustrations are in every case shown full size.

Cover: from *January 1973:11* by Patrick Heron (screenprint)

published in 1979 by
Waddington Galleries Limited
2 Cork Street
London W1X 1PA

ISBN 0 9506567 0 4

designed by Sally Jeffery
printed in Great Britain by
Westerham Press Limited
Westerham, Kent

contents

introduction

The nature of printmaking

The word 'print' is a confusing one because its catchment area is so wide. It may describe the pattern on a frock, typography as well as imagery in newspapers and books, a cheap copy of a Van Gogh painting made photomechanically by a four-colour half-tone process, or the kind of print with which this book is concerned – the work of an artist who has chosen to widen the distribution of an idea by conceiving it especially for one of the four main graphic processes.

An artist's print is not created in the same way as a unique painting, by making direct marks on paper or canvas, but at one remove, by first fashioning what an engineer would call a 'tool' and then using it to produce a series of identical impressions.

To print the simplest line by means of each of the major traditional techniques, the artist must arrange for ink to be conveyed to paper by means of:
i. a ridge in a wood block left standing proud after the surrounding areas have been lowered (a relief print);
ii. an incision either directly cut by a sharp implement or indirectly eroded by acid into the surface of a metal plate (an intaglio print);
iii. a greasemark crayoned or painted onto a slab of porous limestone or a grained alloy plate (a lithograph);
iv. a chink in an open weave fabric stretched on a frame and blocked in the parts not intended to print by a form of stencil (a screenprint).

The resulting work of art is not the 'tool' described, which is simply a means to an end, but the image such a device is able to transfer repeatedly to paper.

The role of prints before photography

To understand contemporary prints – particularly the conventions and prejudices which have grown up around them – one needs to glance back into history, because a radical change of attitude occurred about a century ago. Before photography took over their workaday role, hand-made prints were primarily a way of circulating information, including that about other works of art. Although there have always been a few artists fascinated by and thoroughly involved in printmaking for its own sake (Dürer, Rembrandt and Goya, for example), the great majority of prints produced during the five hundred years that artists in the west have made them, were frankly imitative. Graphic art attempted not to exploit its own characteristics so much as to reproduce the unique media. Engraving imitated pen

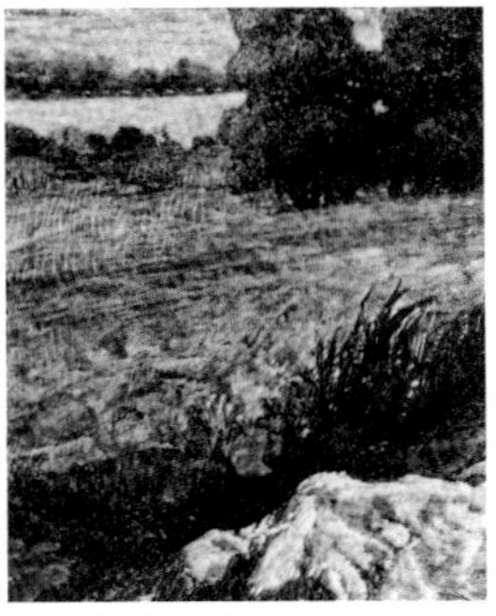

Elbridge Kingsley/wood engraving (detail)

hatching, soft-ground etching mimicked crayon, mezzotint relayed the tones of chiaroscuro oil painting, aquatint evoked water colour washes and wood engravings even pretended to be photographs.

Few pre-nineteenth century practitioners would have dreamed of artificially limiting an edition; indeed, everything possible was done to make the 'tools' last longer. In the mid-nineteenth century however, with the industrial revolution in top gear and a growing well-to-do middle class interested in owning pictures, the Printsellers' Association began the practice of differentiating proofs and artificially limiting editions of reproductions. More and more complex intaglio techniques were used to copy oil paintings which had often been especially made by popular Victorian painters with that end in view. Prints were signed by both originating painter and reproductive engraver, the latter capable of spending several years and not a little of his eyesight hand-cutting the plate. Later in the century, these manual engravers became redundant as photomechanical procedures took over and momentarily it looked as if Landseer's brother had been right when he punned that photography was the 'foe-to-graphic' art.

The establishing of 'originality'

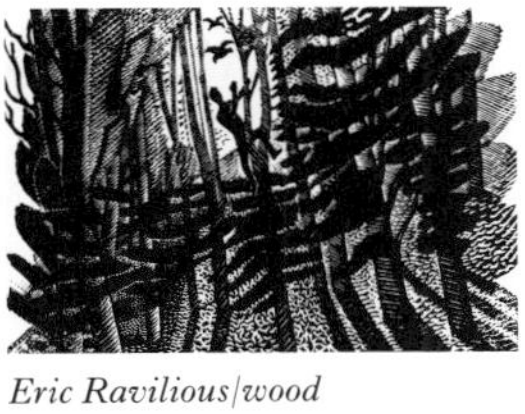

Eric Ravilious/wood engraving

What happened however, was that instead of relying on interpretative engravers, as most had in the past, artists became increasingly interested in using the graphic media themselves. Gradually 'reproduction' once the norm, became a dirty word. Systematic engraving was castigated as 'mindless manufacture' and intuitive and spontaneous etching, owing much to Rembrandt's example, triumphed. The invitation to 'Come up and see my etchings'! (or my original wood-engraved book illustrations) dates from this era and these two processes were dominant until the Depression destroyed the graphic art market between the wars.

Since this activity had arisen in opposition to increasing mechanisation, it is hardly surprising that the kind of image-making that artists themselves developed was what Walter Benjamin has called a 'fetishistic fundamentally anti-technological notion of art'. The deification of the individualised gesture however, in many ways suppressed printmaking's natural potential for wide distribution. Mystique and rarified connoisseurship were encouraged, not least by an elitist art market which, on the whole, still doesn't want to know how to cope with distribution of the mass-produced, or to equate the lower costs increased production makes possible with 'art'.

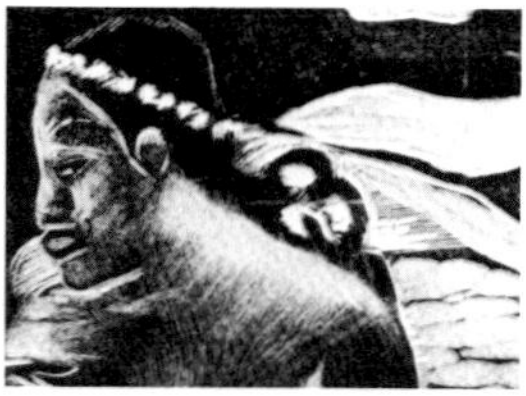

Paul Gauguin/woodcut (detail)

The American artist, Whistler, was the hero of this art for art's sake movement and Gauguin, Munch, and the Brücke artists emulated him in making personalised variations rather than identical editions. Prints were not merely autonomous, they tried to become unique. Whistler created monotype suites from one etching plate suggesting various moods by painterly surface tone, thus helping to establish what the trade from that time has called an 'original print', the ideal in his day being an image in which the concept, the fabrication of the printing 'tool', and very often the printing of all the sheets, was accomplished by one and the same man. Eventually it became the custom to write a serial number on each print, and to artificially limit the edition by cancelling the plate having printed a pre-determined number. This, together with a pencilled signature, conferred aura and uniqueness on each image, authenticating it as a 'relic of the true cross'. Whistler compounded the situation even further in the late 1880s when he issued lithographs, signed and with wide margins, at twice the price of an identical image on smaller paper, unsigned. This suggested matters extrinsic to the subject – an autograph and extra border – were worth as much as its intrinsic qualities, an inversion of values time has done little to correct.

Post-war print growth

After a hiatus in print publishing, caused by financial setback then the second world war, colour lithography emerged as the popular 'original print' medium, morally superior, it was implied, to the cheap four-colour photomechanical reproductions of old masters then widespread. Even lithographs by the most famous artists were marketed at reasonable prices, allowing a genuine belief to develop among idealists that original prints could democratise an artist's work. Even before the war, extremely inexpensive prints on which artists had worked themselves had been produced by the Artists' International Association for working people and by John Piper's Contemporary Lithograph venture for schoolchildren. A vintage Paul Nash published in 1937 cost the equivalent of £14 today.

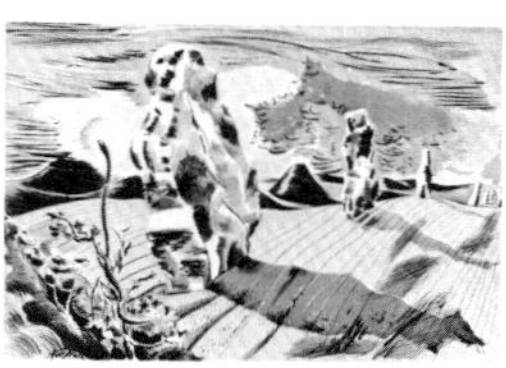

Paul Nash/lithograph

As post-war enthusiasm for the Ecole de Paris grew however, other sectors of the market were less benign. One of the most revealing developments was that although both manual and photographic technicians continued to be used for high quality reproductions, their role was now concealed. Whereas in the nineteenth century a reproduction would be identified as by A (the copyist) after B (the originator), as the twentieth century progressed, A's intervention was rarely disclosed because assumption of the inventor's direct participation was now critically relevant to the print's monetary value. Many artists would hand a readymade gouache to one of the incredibly gifted Parisian lithographic copyists who would do all the work without credit so the publishers could market the signed reproductions and suggest they were originals by confusing terminology. Because the gullible had been taught that signatures automatically indicated direct artistic involvement, disreputable dealers forged them, particularly on the unsigned but often very attractive artists' autographic print insets cheaply distributed in large editions through art periodicals.

Photography and screenprinting

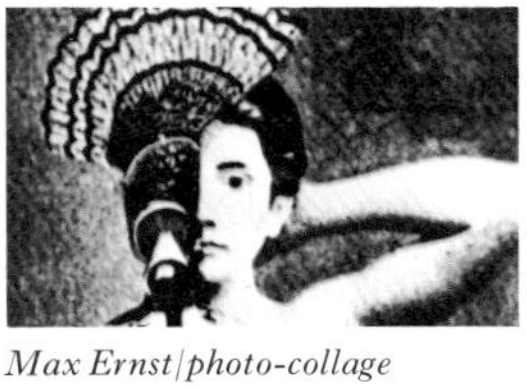

Max Ernst/photo-collage rephotographed (detail)

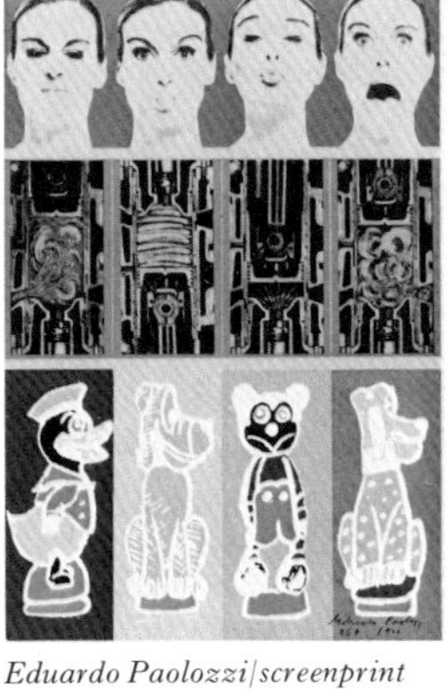

Eduardo Paolozzi/screenprint

For the public trying to find its way among such boobytraps, the confusion of originals with reproductions was exacerbated by the gradual acceptance of the creative use of photo-technology into the art of printmaking during the 1960s. As early as 1920, the Dadaists Max Ernst and Man Ray, had made use of printed photo-collage in their attempts to outrage those bourgeois values still equating art with the hand-made. Earlier, Marcel Duchamp had placed mass-produced machine-made articles which he called 'ready-mades' into an aesthetic context, asserting that they became 'art' through his intellectual choice, incidentally divorcing concept from craft skill.

By the early 1960s screenprinting, a twentieth-century print technique which infiltrated its way from commerce into fine art in America during the late 1930s, became the medium through which photographic images finally entered avant-garde orthodoxy. Andy Warhol and Robert Rauschenberg incorporated them into paintings from 1961 and once the tendency grew for Pop artists to poetically assemble pre-processed imagery from disparate media sources in their work, it was hardly relevant any longer to insist they should make it by hand. A genus of prints therefore emerged no longer 'original' (in the traditional sense of the artist grappling with all the materials personally) but not adequately to be defined as reproductions either. For the printer would act in most cases not by copying a pre-existing work of art, but upon written instructions, rough graph-paper diagrams, or collages which the artist wished to integrate onto a single plane by means of process; creative screen-prints were also arrived at experimentally by the trial and error mutation of stage proofs. Thus an extensive collaborative relationship grew up between printer and artist, analogous to that between builder and architect or musician and composer, allowing craft traditions to be extended by a growingly sophisticated print technology.

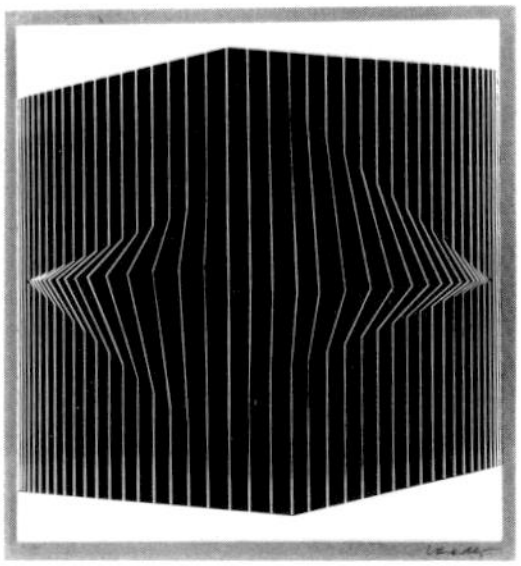

Victor Vasarely/screenprint

This pro-technological spirit also had roots in Constructivism, for in addition to the Pop artists' interest in screenprinting, its cool mechanised perfection was attractive to those using the hard-edged precision geometries of perceptual abstraction. While it may be questionable for an artist whose force resides in idiosyncratic gesture to delegate that gesture to others, it became less important who cut the stencil for a red square.

Hand versus machine

These developments were not accepted, of course, without considerable reactionary backlash and between 1960 and 1965 the Viennese International Congress of Plastic Arts, the Print Council of America and a French national committee, sought both semantically and ethically to define an original print in traditional terms. Since by this time some artists even painted by proxy, the definitions seemed destined to close the cage after the bird had flown. The situation was not entirely academic, however, and temporarily affected tax and import laws. In Britain before VAT was introduced, ironic legislation allowed printed 'art' (defined as that in editions up to 75 copies) to be tax free, while 'reproductions' (anything in editions larger than 75) were subject to a heavy 'fancy goods' tax. Thus a Socialist government safe-guarded the connoisseur market while attacking imaginative print publishing ventures then trying once more to get inexpensive artists' prints and multiples to a wider public. On the whole, artists, where they could get publishers to support them, did as they wished, but an intriguing hedging of bets, especially in the prints produced during the second half of the 1960s, can be detected in the tensions set up between mechanical (i.e. photographic) marks and those hand made.

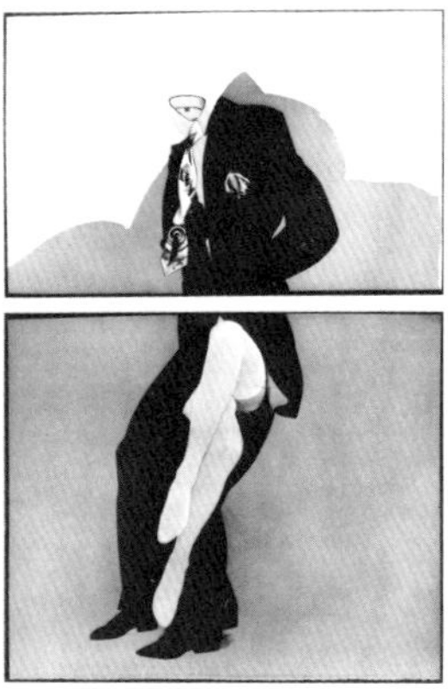

Allen Jones/litho and photo-litho

Book-keeping versus aesthetics

The American print historian William Ivins said that one should concentrate on the intellectual and imaginative background of great prints – the rest was book-keeping, and one takes his point. Yet such an attitude suggests that the history of art is a succession of self-contained technical and stylistic developments unrelated to society and perpetuates the myth that art, as a division of high culture, is beyond financial, ideological and political concerns. In fact, detailing the machinations of the print market (symbolically banished to the end of this text) reveals how far dealers and artists have gone this century to maintain art as an esoteric confine and status-conferring commodity for circulation only to the comparatively rich.

The Belgian artist, Marcel Broodthaers, who defined printmaking as 'market study', expressed the situation with transparent lucidity in the two-sheet screenprint *Poème-Change-Exchange-Wechsel*. The 'poem' consists of serried ranks – editions – of his signatures, which after being pooled together in a bureau-de-change are then re-issued as deutschmarks, francs, pounds and dollars. Inevitably the print was made in a limited edition and connoisseurs delightedly consume it in esoteric gallery environments.

It would be easy to write off printmaking, publishing and dealing in cynical terms as nothing more than the inevitable tendency for capitalism to turn everything first and foremost into a commodity. The paradox is that in this century, allegedly of the common man, artists have elaborated printmaking to the point where content and technique inseparably combine in a way capable of communicating the most subtle aesthetic ideas to a vastly extended audience; that they have simultaneously also deliberately limited that humane and subversive potential need not be the end of the story.

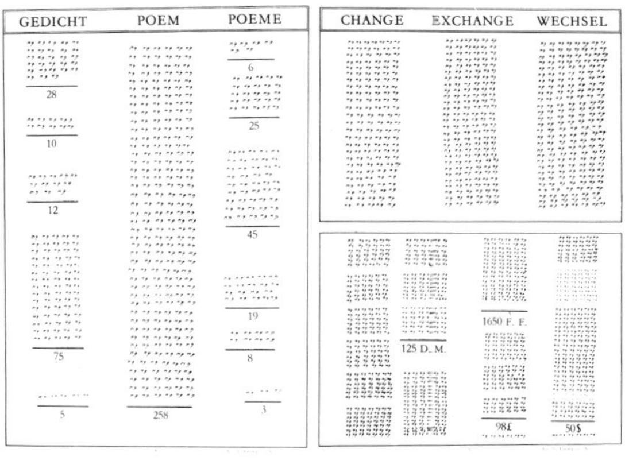

Marcel Broodthaers/screenprint

relief printing

'In order that the point may enter the world (like a fortress with a ditch)' wrote Kandinsky about woodcut, 'it is necessary to do violence to its entire surroundings, to tear them out and destroy them.'

It is the principle of relief printing that the ink is applied to the original surface of the block after the parts not wanted have been cut away. This is also the principle upon which a potato cut or a rubber date stamp functions. Since letterpress, which is relief typography, was paramount until this century, relief images have always been thought ideal for book illustration because they were what is called 'type-compatible'. Indeed, block books, with text and pictures entirely cut from wood, were the earliest form of western printed book, dating together with religious images and playing cards, from the fifteenth century. At this time the artist probably drew his design direct on the wood and then had a facsimile of the line cut by a craftsman. Dürer was probably the greatest artist ever to make relief prints and it is thought he may have cut some of his blocks personally. Because the amount of detail possible was limited, prints from metal eventually ousted wood except for the cruder ballad sheets and broadsheets aimed at the less sophisticated lower classes.

A major technical step was taken in the late eighteenth century by Thomas Bewick who, instead of using the traditional knife and gouge on plank wood, developed wood engraving by using metal engraving tools on the end or cross-grain. This, together with finer papers and rollers instead of dabbers to apply the ink, not to mention his meticulous presswork, permitted much more detailed pictures. These wood engravings used not only the traditional black line, but white marks removed out of the black mass, thought out in terms of the various tools themselves. This discovery was used for the illustration of news magazines and books as growing numbers of people learnt to read during the nineteenth century. So much detail was packed in by specialised cutters copying artists' drawings or even attempting to rival photography by hand, that towards the end of the nineteenth century, Gauguin protested that wood engraving had become 'like photogravure . . . detestable'.

The first photo-mechanical blocks were in fact deep etched metal cuts printed from the relief surface. Aubrey Beardsley designed brilliantly for them in the 1890s. The main tendency among artists however, as photomechanics spread, was anti-technological. Gauguin and the Norwegian artist Edvard Munch embodied in their woodcuts lessons they had learned from Japanese colour prints and other more primitive sources. They were emulated by two early twentieth-century Expressionist groups – the Fauves and the Brücke – who also reverted to the use of knife and gouge on plank, no longer relying on craftsmen. The stronghold of the relief print between the wars remained the illustrated book, for which white line wood engravings were provided by artists themselves. Bibliophiles were shocked to their very core in 1900 when Bonnard illustrated a book with pink lithographs!

After the second world war, relief prints finally escaped from their literary connections and like most other artists' prints became much larger coloured wall objects. Under the influence of abstraction and the continuing example of subtle printing by contemporary Japanese, artists like Michael Rothenstein exploited all manner of found surfaces – tree trunk, weathered plank, or metal scrap. As the American Ed Casarella commented: 'If you can ink it you can print it!' An altogether new grandeur of scale was attempted.

Since then, other materials from cardboard to plastics, have been pressed into service. Lino, first used in the 1920s was taken over by Picasso, already a septuagenarian, in the late 1950s. With his customary inventiveness he generated entirely novel ways of cutting and colouring the block.

While traditional prints can usually be clearly defined as relief or intaglio, the practice of printing simultaneously from the surface as well as from the indentations in a plate or block have blurred these formerly discrete categories. Eric Gill realised as early as 1924 that a wood engraving could be inked on the surface as a relief print or in the incisions like an etching.

An extension of this principle is the American collagraph, where a variety of objects glued to a base plate may be printed simultaneously from the heights and the depths.

woodcut

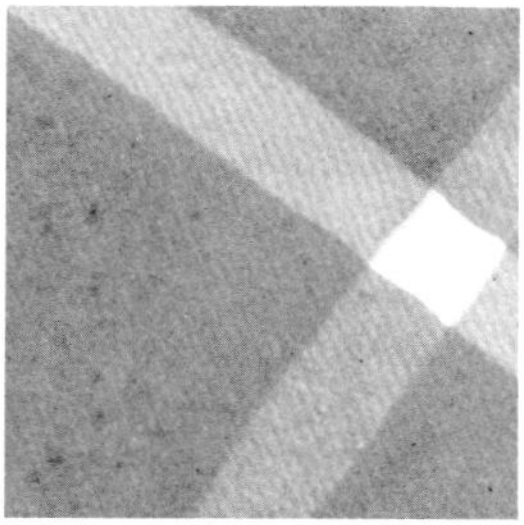

The prints of Kim Lim, wife of the sculptor William Turnbull, have always shown acute sensitivity to the interaction of particular inks from particular surfaces on particular supports – in this case a deckle-edged sheet of paper hand made by the Japanese.

Although André Malraux claimed that photography, by relaying works of art through reproduction, had created a 'museum without walls', in fact the qualities possessed by this deceptively simple print are virtually irreproducible, stemming entirely from the nature of the chosen materials themselves. No reproduction will make it possible to see the way one ink layer merges with another, both being absorbed by the exquisite paper, the feel of which is as soft as a well laundered cambric handkerchief.

Repeatability is the essence of printing and the same block has been overprinted twice to create the image, having been turned through 90 degrees for the second printing, hence the title *Spin* which suggests whirling rotation. The intense saturation of the warm marigold colour makes the tiny square at the centre of the printed blocks appear to gleam more whitely than the surrounding paper, while successive layers of colour sitting transparently over one another suggest the nestling petals of a flower, seen against the light.

Kim Lim's prints make one aware how far knowledge about something from a reproduction may be from direct sensuous acquaintance with the original. This is the crux of the difference between the artist controlling all the determinants in a print and a print in which an original is interpreted by other people.

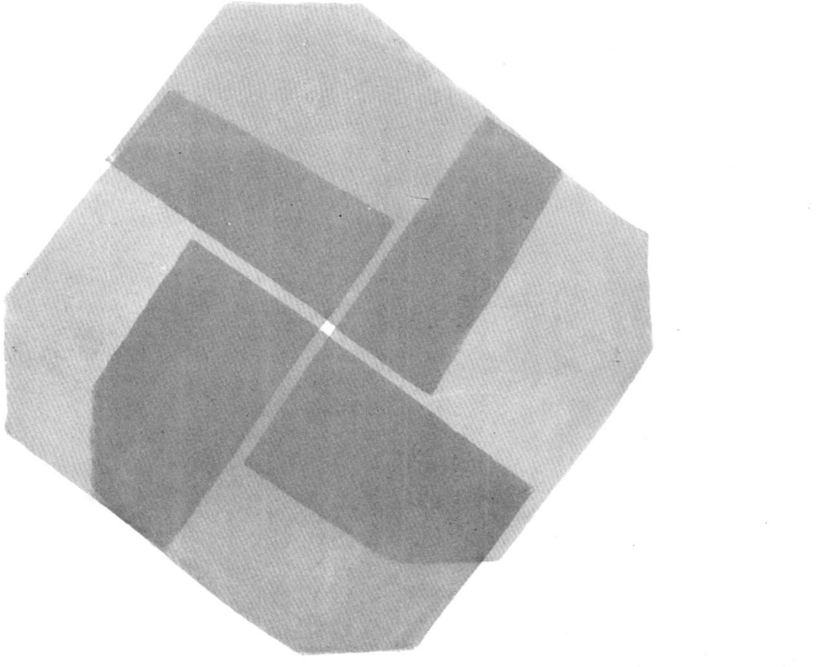

Kim Lim (b. 1936)

Spin 1974
woodcut on Japanese paper
$17\frac{1}{2}'' \times 22\frac{3}{4}''$/44.5 × 57.8 cm
edition 8
published by Waddington Graphics

wood engraving

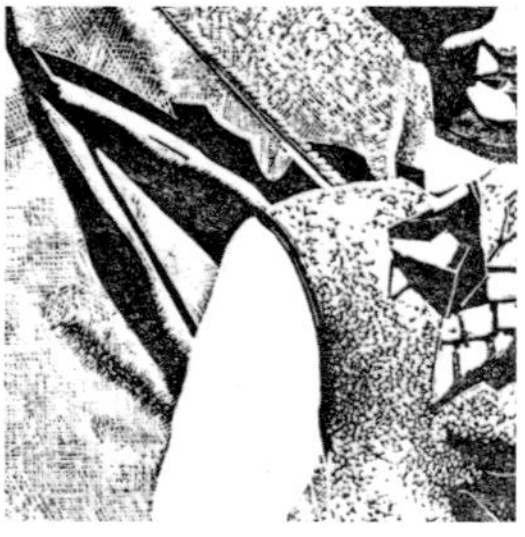

As a young Pop artist in the 1960s, Peter Blake questioned the necessity for life drawing, infiltrated hitherto unacceptable images from popular culture into fine art and did his share of kicking against the traces. Currently however, in completing a suite of wood engravings of circus freaks, he has been conscious of 'picking up a relay baton' and accepting the challenge to perpetuate a craft tradition that has almost died out.

While Blake was at art school it was still the custom during the last year of intermediate to try one's hand at one of the crafts – silversmithing, lettering or wood engraving. So he remembered 'vestiges of information' and, together with a look at the wood-engraved work done earlier this century by artists such as Edward Gordon Craig and John Farleigh, was prepared for his attempt. The fine cutting of hairlines and tiny stippled dots is so exhausting and taxing to both hand and eye however, that the making of the five prints was spread over five years. They have been editioned by White Ink in a neutral ink on off-white paper, rather than harsh black and white.

His image sources were picture postcards made from copies of *Illustrated London News* in the 1870s, showing circus people such as bearded ladies, fat boys, giants and dwarfs. Thus Blake has been reinterpreting Victorian reproductive wood engravings, reaction to which set artists scurrying off to cut their own wood blocks at the turn of the century. Their white line engravings became all the rage for the illustration of private press books as well as providing a range of enchanting small pictures for the home. As Campbell Dodgson wrote for the first annual exhibition of the Society of Wood Engravers in 1920, wood engravings made 'an excellent effect in the decoration of small rooms such as most of the world inhabits in days when the burden of taxes is heavy'. As a general rule, this heavily taxed world has since opted for large scale and colour.

Perhaps the greatest achievement of the wood engraver John Farleigh, whom Blake mentions among his mentors, was to circulate his most beautiful wood engravings widely in inexpensive unlimited edition books. As a challenge, it could certainly provide another baton for art's relay race.

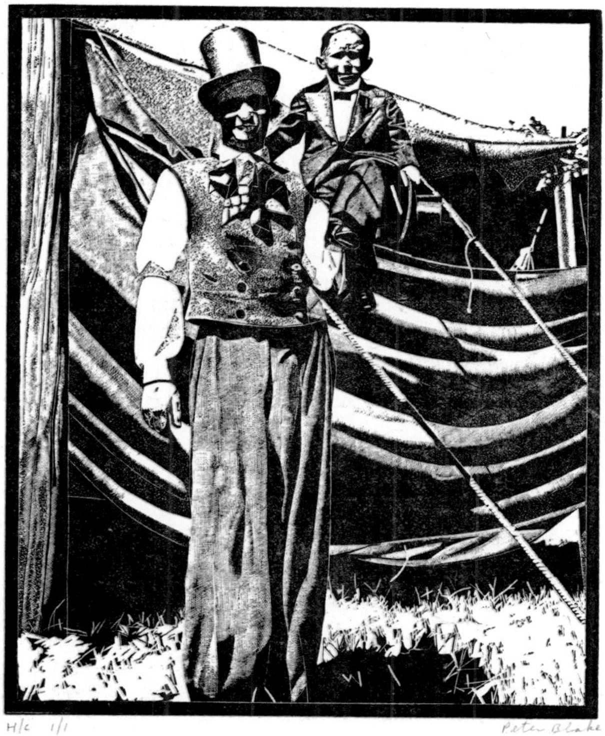

Peter Blake (b.1932)

Giant from *Side Show* 1974/78
11″ × 9″/27.9 × 22.9 cm
wood engraving
edition 100 + 30 artist's proofs
published by Waddington Graphics

linocut

In 1945, after the war, Picasso made a great many lithographs at the Atelier Mourlot in Paris. Upon his move to the south of France in the 1950s however, the delays he experienced waiting for proofs made him impatiently turn to a printer called Arnera, closer at hand in Vallauris, who had linocut a poster for him.

Lino, a floor covering made of a thick coating of oxidised linseed oil on a coarse cloth backing, was used by a few British artists, such as Claude Flight and his circle, in the 1920s. Because of its cheapness most schoolchildren have made prints with it.

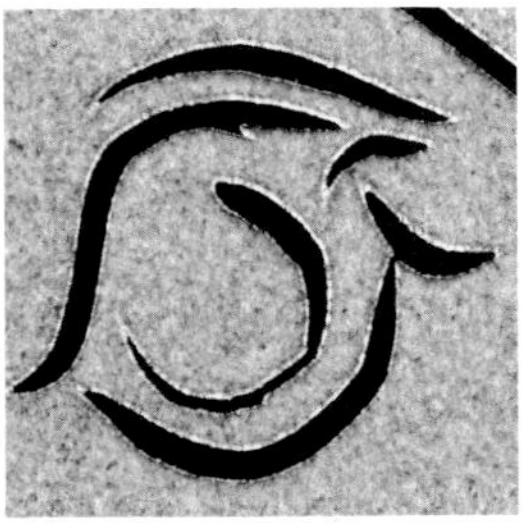

Picasso radically transformed the medium. In some cuts he delighted in the broad and obvious marks of the gouge, in others he made the most subtle tonal use of a surface lightly grazed with the multiple tool. In the one illustrated, he has circumvented the need to remove all the material on either side of a black line by printing from the entire surface of the block inked in black and then overprinting the same block in greyish white, having removed the image from it as a single line cut. One needs infinite control to create a line with such apparent effortlessness in resistant material.

Ideas from the slip treatment of pottery in earth colours, which he was then undertaking, invade his work in lino. The move back to the Mediterranean revived many Arcadian themes and his continuing fascination with still lives, portraits, as well as his renewed passion for the bullfight, form the bulk of his subjects.

In the image shown, a picador has broken his lance when plunging it into the neck of the bull to weaken it. Perhaps only Picasso (or Goya?) could convince an Anglo Saxon of the poetry in this bloodthirsty ritual, by transforming an image of impending death into a line of elegant almost neoclassical simplicity.

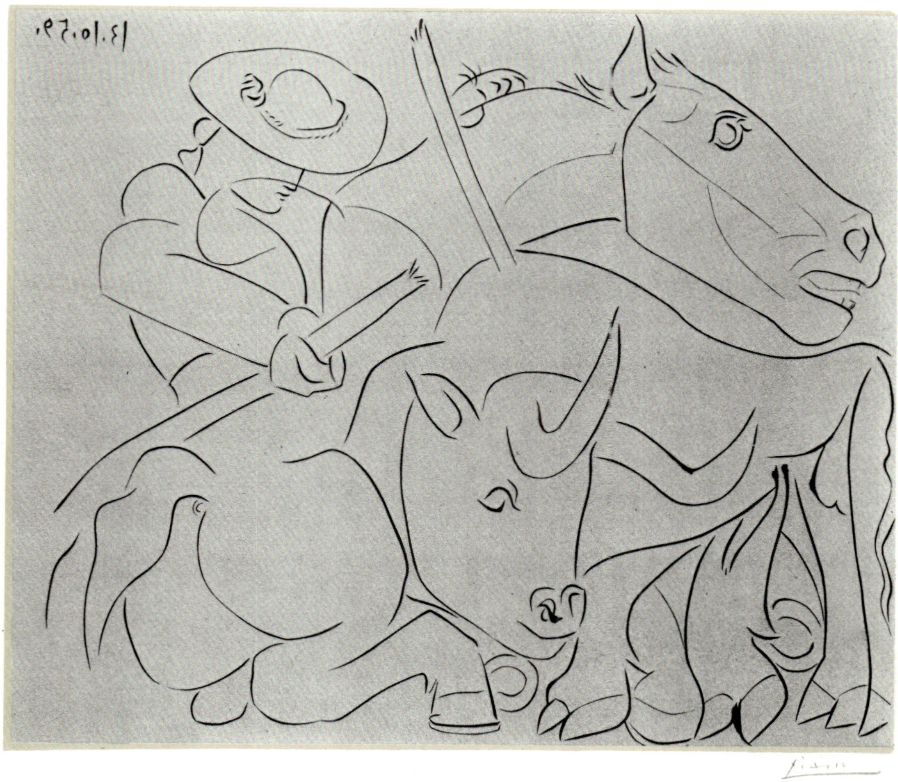

Pablo Picasso (1881–1973)

La Pique Cassée dated 13.10.59 (Bloch 921)
two colour linocut
$24\frac{1}{2}'' \times 29\frac{3}{4}''$/62.2 × 75.6 cm
edition 50
published by Mourlot

intaglio printing

The intaglio process is a method of printing not from the surface, but from the incisions in a metal plate. These incisions can be made either directly by an implement which cuts the metal (engraving, drypoint, mezzotint) or less laboriously and indirectly by protecting parts of the plate and allowing acid to erode certain exposed areas (etching, aquatint). A stiff ink is applied over the whole surface of the plate, and is then traditionally wiped clean from the surface but left in the crevices. From these it is sucked out into dampened paper under heavy pressure from a rolling press not unlike a domestic mangle. The depth of the cut or the length of the acid's bite affect the amount of ink that can be held in the incision and thus the 'colour' of the line. Under pressure from the press this line becomes a raised cast of damp paper surmounted by ink, while the platemark is permanently embossed into the sheet. This is the hallmark of an intaglio print, although some artists who have wanted to escape its insistent rectangularity – Miro, for example – have made it disappear by using a plate larger than the sheet of paper, or, like Ben Nicholson, have cut and shaped the plate irregularly.

It is thought that engraving as a print form was developed when metalsmiths took proofs of incised designs on armour or niello ornaments. At first artists worked with the burin or the drypoint tool directly on metal. Later, etching, known early in the sixteenth century but not fully developed until the seventeenth, reduced the labour necessary by allowing chemistry to take over from muscle power. Both techniques were often employed together in the same plate. Because an intaglio print could carry more information per square inch than woodcut, intaglio prints superseded relief prints until Bewick's discoveries made wood viable again, although intaglio prints have always been more difficult and more costly to print.

Several artists of the Renaissance engraved their plates themselves – among them Mantegna, Pollaiuolo and Dürer. Others employed engravers to popularise their work for them; Raphael, for example, used the services of Marcantonio Raimondi. His reproductive engraving established certain conventions and a systematic way of laying lines. Our modern emphasis on spontaneity and originality has tended to push such formal work into the shade, complaining of its mechanistic impersonality. Others, attuned to recent systemic disciplines in fine art, have begun to look again at a whole body of work the nineteenth century ruled as of no possible interest.

Etching, which at first was regarded as a way of imitating engraving, found its greatest exponent in Rembrandt, in many ways a forerunner of more recent experimental attitudes and a hero to the modern movement. In the hands of such a master, printmaking is no longer a minor or derivative medium secondary to an artist's unique output, but as important a means of expression and one that may well have absorbed an equal share of his time.

As the medium taken up by the 'original print' brigade, etching became hierarchically and snobbishly speaking, the most important of the print media. As William Ivins put it . . . 'there was a strongly and generally held opinion that etching was more artistic than line engraving, that both were more artistic than wood engravings, that wood engraving was more artistic than wood-cutting, and that all were more artistic than lithography. Lowest of all and utterly contemptible were photography and any medium that bore the name of some process.'

One of the great technical wizards of intaglio printing was S W Hayter who opened an atelier in Paris in the 1920s which evacuated to America during the second world war, enormously extending his influence. He pioneered a number of discoveries concerning simultaneous colour printing by the use of different viscosities of ink deposited at various levels in the intaglio plate; through him, the intaglio print became a colour-carrying sculptural relief embossed into the paper. He was a purist when it came to originality and an oracle when it came to information: Picasso and Jackson Pollock were among many artists he advised.

Photo-process as it first developed meant etching away the unwanted parts, then printing from the relief surface. Photogravure was a nineteenth century intaglio process for transferring a photographic image to metal plate and etching it in. Such images were specifically outlawed from 'original' printing until as recently as 1965. Since photography became respectable however, photographs have been regularly incorporated into all kinds of intaglio print.

etching and engraving

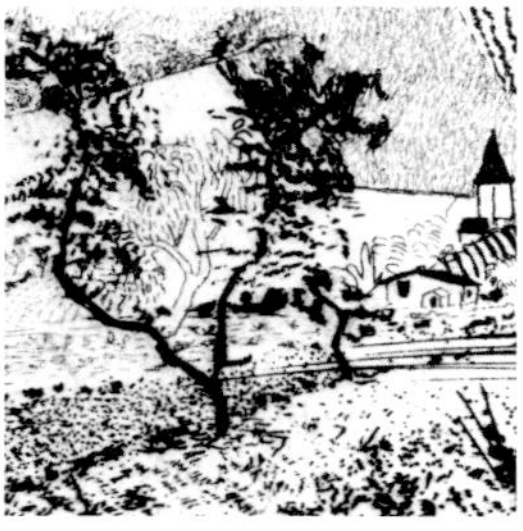

Tony Gross, for many years teacher of printmaking at the Slade School of Art, was one of the few painter-etchers good enough to survive the failure of the print market after the Depression. Although still a painter and one who as an official war artist recorded the second world war in watercolour with vivacity, his international fame rests chiefly on his graphic work. In it, a gay and lyrical line is applied to landscape or to humorous and sympathetic studies featuring the daily life of ordinary people. Rejecting colour and maintaining one could get as much as one needed from black and white, his forté has lain in inventive and spontaneous drawing. In this exquisite scene at Pujols it ranges from grass so fine and delicate that one marvels a man's hand could draw it, to the clustered leaves on trees for which the encrustations from progressively deeper biting suggest the darker masses.

While etching allows one to draw freely and cursively in this way with only the force needed to scratch or penetrate wax, engraving, which means directing the cutting implement into the resistant surface of zinc or copper, needs greater control. The cut must be made in a direction away from the body, the whole plate being swung if a curve is attempted. The respective marks of etching versus engraving can perhaps be compared to skywriting versus the path of a skate through ice. The engraved line can consequently usually be distinguished from that in an etching by virtue of its economy, incisiveness and sense of direction.

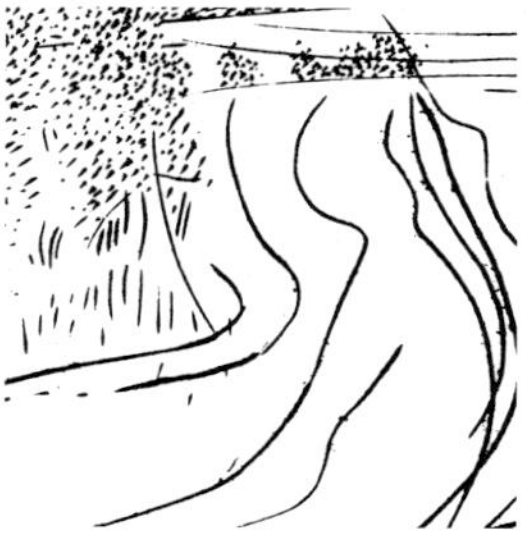

Although the bulk of Gross's printed output has been etched, a few early plates from 1929/30 were engraved and recently he took up the burin again for this concise depiction direct on the metal of a field near Le Boulvé in France – a village in which he lives for the summer months of each year. The tangled stems of grass at the edge of the field around which two butterflies play stereoscopically, are seen against the austere lines of an autumnal stubble field. These recede and lose themselves amidst distant vegetation rendered by a powdering of stippled dots.

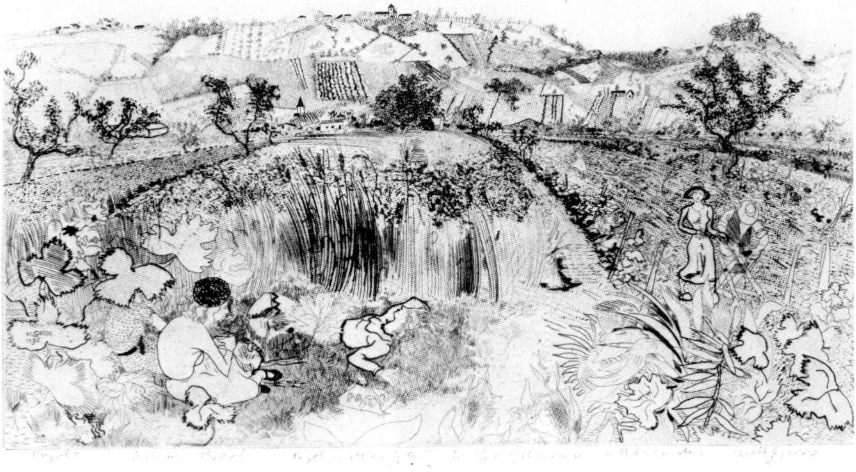

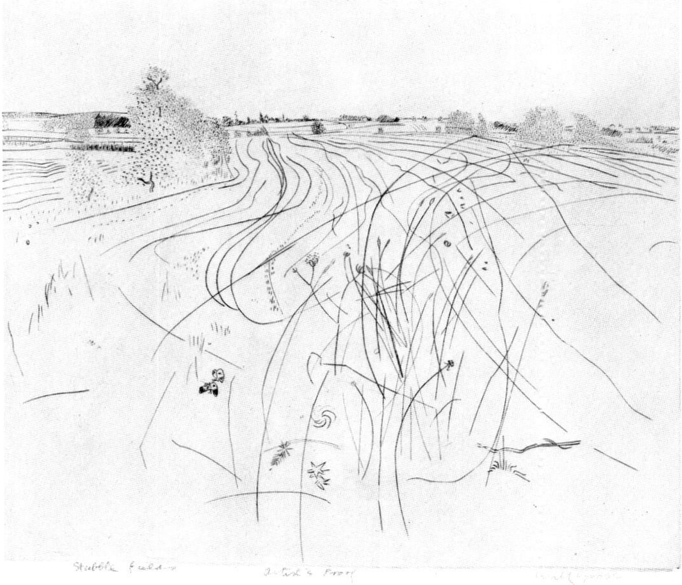

Anthony Gross (b. 1905)

△ *Pujols* 1932
etching
14″ × 17″/35.6 × 43.2 cm
Image size $7\frac{5}{8}$″ × $11\frac{1}{2}$″/19.4 × 29.3 cm
edition 50
published by the artist

▽ *Stubble Fields* 1975
engraving
14″ × $20\frac{1}{4}$″/35.6 × 51.4 cm
image size $8\frac{3}{4}$″ × $10\frac{1}{2}$″/22.2 × 26.7 cm
edition 50
published by Bernard Jacobson Limited

drypoint

Like engraving, this is a direct method of working using a hard steel or diamond point. It forces the copper or zinc up into a burr on one or both sides of the incised furrow, depending on the inclination at which the implement is held. When inked the metal projections cannot be wiped as clean as the surrounding plate and this gives the drypoint line its characteristic velvety bleed. The burr wears fast under pressure from the press. At the beginning of this century artists like Helleu and Jacques Villon loved to use the tool to suggest the furs worn by fashionable women. Throughout the history of the intaglio print it has been a useful means of adding swift emphasis to an etched plate without the bother of immersing the work in the acid bath again.

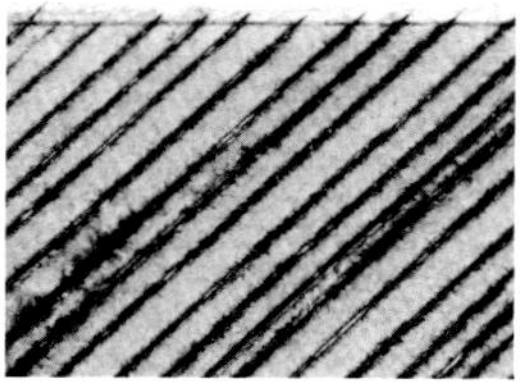

The unusual example illustrated is ninth and last in a suite of self-generating prints made by the abstract painter Alan Green. Beginning with two large rectangular plates he systematically reduced their size, halving one and quartering the other, but using each division of both plates at least three times during the making of the series. The paper size remained constant throughout.

The artist has a free and inventive approach to intaglio markmaking, using the metal almost as if he were drawing and erasing on paper, and allowing changes to the previous state of the image to cause the identity of the next. Copper can withstand such treatment better than paper, although to erase an intaglio mark once it has been bitten in acid or engraved, may mean many hours of work with sanding discs, burnishers and snakestones.

The suite exhausted the entire intaglio repertoire, incorporating mezzotint, aquatint, engraving, drypoint and even a nylon texture applied to a plate through a soft ground. Much of the subtlety of the images came from a hard won knowledge of how printing inks react, gained by working with Tom Freeth and Paul Bristow at Ravensbourne College of Art.

This final image in the suite is printed from a quarter of one of the original plates in which a black ink wiped into drypoint diagonals bursts its way at the moment of printing through a superimposition of white copperplate ink screenprinted onto the surface of the plate.

Alan Green (b.1932)

$\frac{1}{4}$ *Black Diagonal* from the suite *Four to One* 1976
mixed media including drypoint
$27\frac{3}{4}'' \times 33\frac{3}{8}''$/70.5 × 84.8 cm
image size $10\frac{3}{4}'' \times 13\frac{3}{4}''$/27.3 × 34.9 cm
edition 20
published by Annely Juda Fine Art

mezzotint

While drypoint and engraving are direct ways of achieving line on metal, mezzotint is a direct method for achieving tone. The whole of the plate is subliminally pitted with tiny indentations that give the metal a 'tooth' and thus hold ink. Its beauty as a way of rendering a charcoal-like darkness comes from the fact that it not only indents the plate (as aquatinting does with less work) but like the burr on drypoint throws up tiny points which can also hold ink. Once this cellular ink-holding structure has been laboriously 'rocked' all over the metal by means of a curved serrated blade, so that the plate would print a uniform black, the artist selectively scrapes and burnishes back lights and half lights, smoothing some areas so they retain relatively less ink.

Discovered in the 1640s, mezzotint was used chiefly by a school of engravers a century later who popularised Reynolds' oil portraits of society beauties. John Martin and Turner both mezzotinted plates themselves, although the medium was used chiefly reproductively in the nineteenth century. It was during the post-war period that artists, following the example of Merlyn Evans at the Central School of Art in London, revived mezzotint for original work.

The tiny illustrated windowscape by Dorothea Wight is a perfect recent example of the technique, at its most evocative. A mysterious grey green shadowy landscape is glimpsed through a Venetian blind which has been added in silver by an etched plate.

Dorothea runs Studio Prints in London as an editioning business printing plates for other people. Since 1972 she has won prizes at three international print biennales. Small in scale, but infinitely appealing, her mezzotint cost only £15 when it was first published. It represents the kind of bargain available to those with more sense than money. In a world where print prices are now sky high, it certainly gives credibility to the idea that art could circulate to a wider range of people.

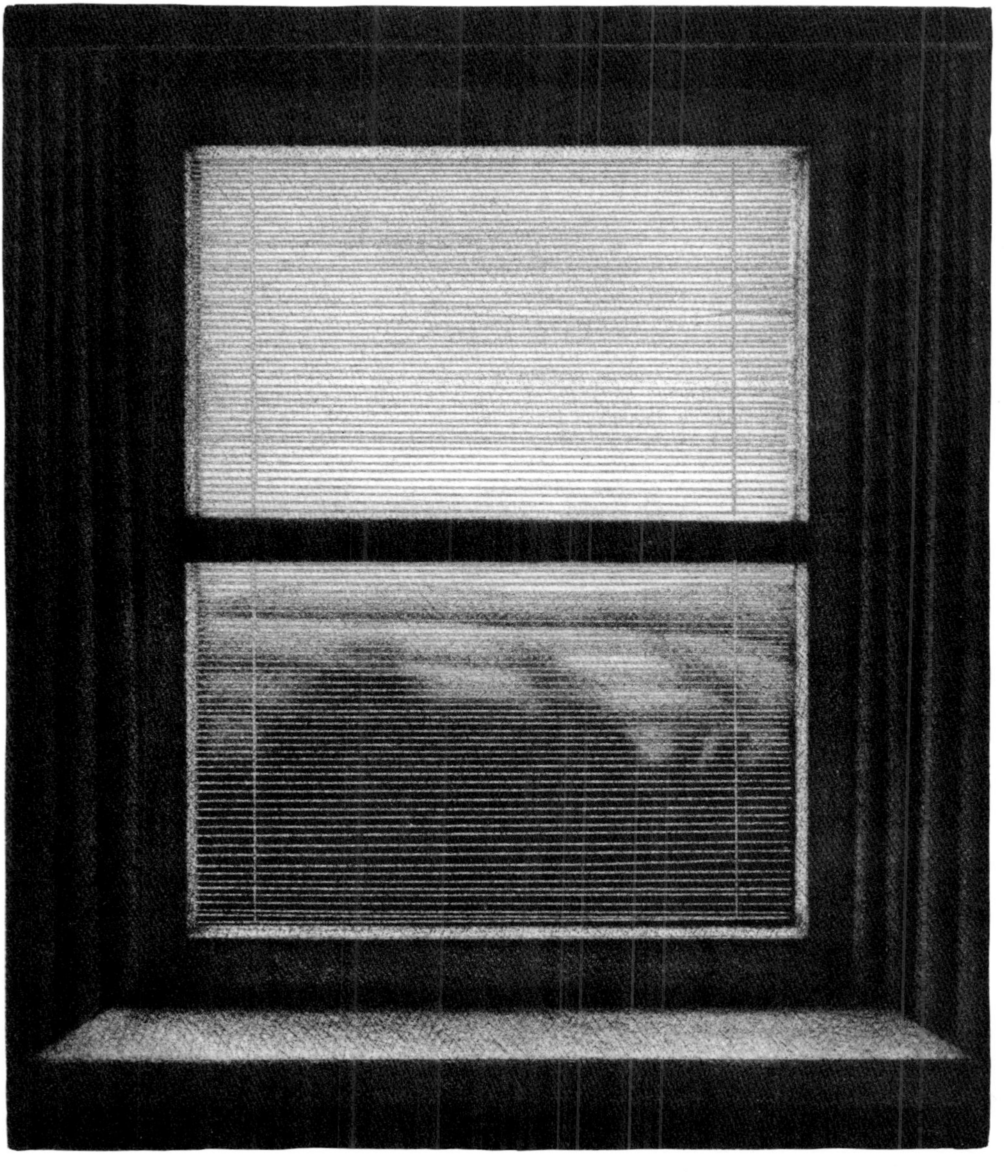

Dorothea Wight (b.1944)

Window with blind 1975
mezzotint with etching
13″ × 11″/33 × 27.9 cm
image size 6″ × 5¼″/15.2 × 13.3 cm
edition 50
published by the artist

hard ground and soft ground etching

Etching was perfected in Germany during the first quarter of the sixteenth century. Made first on iron, which rusted, copper was later found to be the best metal for it, although zinc and steel are also used. Instead of the intaglio incision being made directly by the burin, acid does the work. An acid-resisting ground, waxy in nature, is applied to the plate. The artist draws through it with an etching needle to expose the metal. The plate is then immersed in an acid bath which attacks only the exposed lines, producing incisions corresponding to the drawing without any of the hard labour associated with engraving. Fine lines can be 'stopped out' with varnish early on, while protracted biting creates a deeper incision able to carry a heavier charge of ink.

Soft ground is a variant of etching in which tallow or vaseline is added to a standard ground to make it tacky. Into this covering applied to the plate various textures can be pressed, pushing the ground aside in faithful echo of their pattern. The ground can also be covered with paper before it is drawn into. The drawn line exposes the metal by lifting the ground on the paper, achieving a softer and more crumbly line which, when the metal is bitten, assumes the paper's texture.

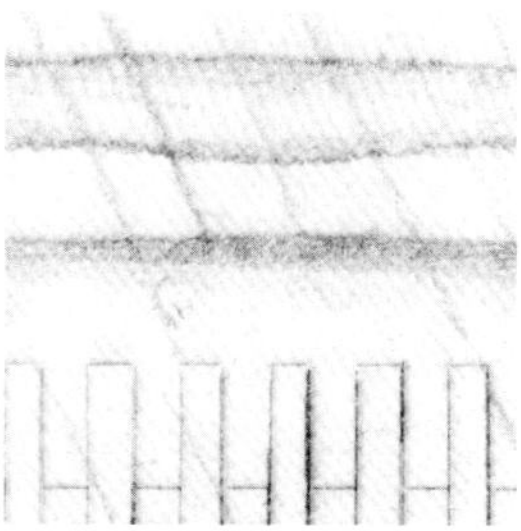

Norman Stevens makes delightful use of both kinds of ground in this picture of a beach house under rain. Following a trip to America in the mid 1960s he painted and etched a number of beautiful images which juxtaposed formalised or geometrically simple architecture with the organic fronds of palms or other vegetation. While the building and fronds here are crisply drawn and etched, the clouded sky, distant foliage, roof shadow and a light smir of rain have been drawn into a soft ground to give them an appropriately delicate character.

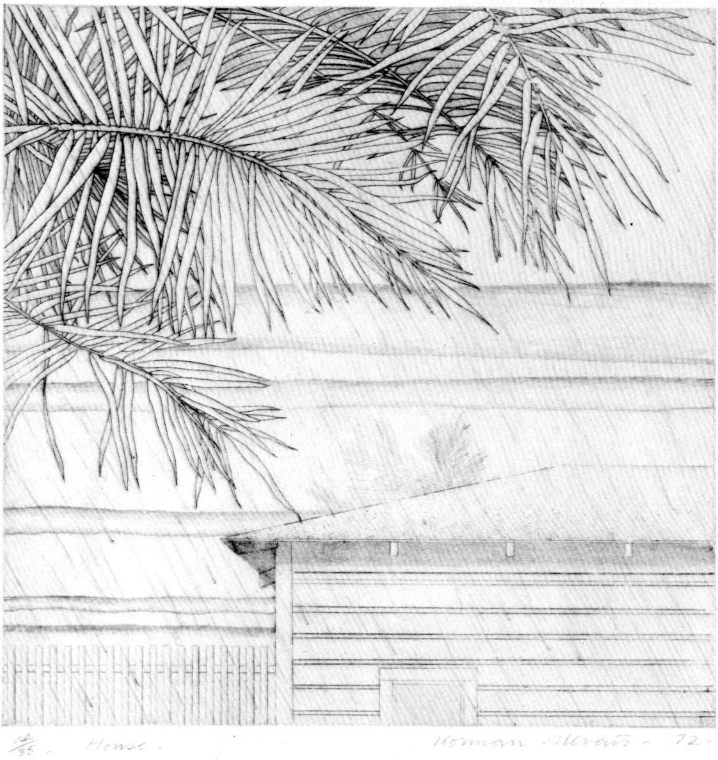

Norman Stevens (b.1937)

Beach House – Rain 1972
hard and soft ground etching
$17\frac{5}{8}'' \times 15\frac{7}{8}''$/44.8 × 40.3 cm
image size $11\frac{7}{8}'' \times 11\frac{1}{2}''$/30.2 × 29.2 cm
edition 35
published by William Weston Gallery

aquatint

Just as etching is a way of incising a line by the use of acid and without the effort of pushing a burin through metal, so aquatint is a way of producing tone without hours of work with a mezzotint rocker. Acid etches around a finely grained resist of resin dust which is shaken all over the plate and is then fused there by heat. The minute particles protect tiny islands of metal while the interstices between them are bitten as a crazing of incisions which will later hold ink. The protective grain can be invisibly fine, or so coarse that it imparts an obvious texture. It is cleaned away by a solvent after the plate has been bitten in acid, but before it is printed. If the plate were to be exposed to acid without a dusting of resin, only the edges of any area thus bitten would hold ink. The dust particles permit an ink-holding roughness to be etched in. It is normal with aquatint to lay the dust all over the plate and then varnish the parts one does not want to print. This means working negatively. A light tone requires a short period in the acid, a darker tone a longer one, so that length of bite controls colour graduation.

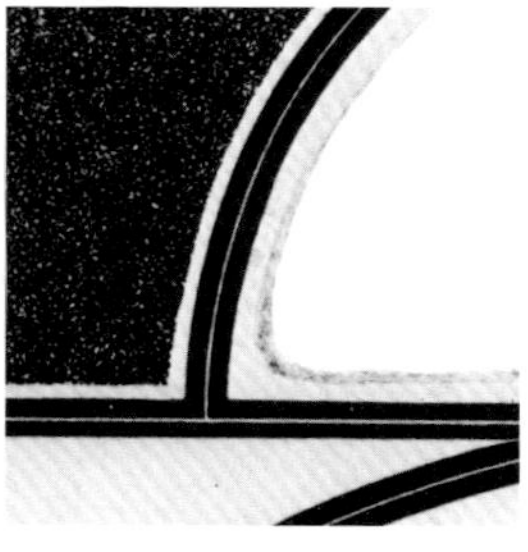

The artist Gordon House, apart from painting, works both as typographic consultant and printmaker. The disciplined grids he uses in typography often invade his image-making, as in the work illustrated, where a simple rectilinear division of 'rigid restraint' is further divided by four arcs. The fine dividing lines and an arc in one area have been aquatinted, while a quadrant within another has been cut right out of the metal, causing embossing in the heavy textured cream paper 'a device used to bring an added dimension and colour to a single printing'.

Thus the dark grid and quadrant, and a pale veil of surface ink extending, except where punctuated by a segment of the original paper, to the plate's bevel, give subtle variety and richness to an otherwise simple and austere image.

The edition was printed at White Ink and the 'chop' or embossed stamp 'HW' in the bottom right hand corner combines the initials of artist and studio.

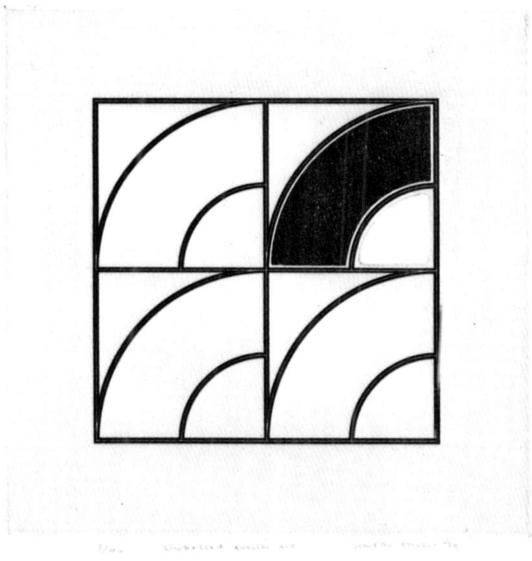

Gordon House (b.1932)

Embossed Quartered Arc 1970
aquatint and embossing
$22'' \times 15\frac{3}{8}''/55.9 \times 39.1$ cm
image size $9\frac{3}{4}'' \times 9\frac{3}{4}''/24.8 \times 24.8$ cm
edition 40
published by Waddington Graphics

sugar or lift ground aquatint

Aquatinting not only means mark-making at one remove (making, as in all prints, not the mark itself but the means to create it) but drawing round that mark negatively and reversing it as a mirror image.

It's not surprising in these circumstances that someone should have devised a positive method of making aquatint marks, permitting an artist to paint or draw directly with brush or pen so that only reversal in printing has to be allowed for.

As with normal aquatint, the plate is resin dusted all over and on that base a positive drawing is made by the artist in a sugary ink which never completely dries. A varnish is then laid over the whole plate including the artist's ink drawing. Immersed in water, the sugary drawing under the varnish swells and lifts, exposing the aquatint grain on the plate so it can be bitten round with acid in the normal way. The remaining varnish protects the rest of the plate.

Gainsborough was one of the first distinguished artists to use the process, able to set down his trees positively much as he would have done in a wash drawing, rather than paint the areas around them. This gestural immediacy has obviously been a key factor in 'original' printmaking, Rouault having been one of the more remarkable users of the medium in France.

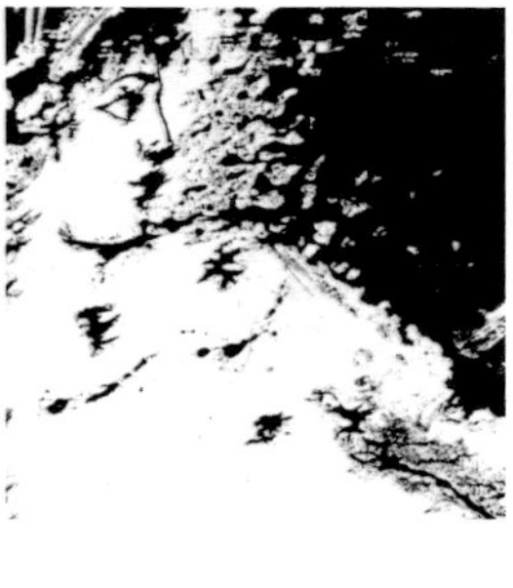

Perhaps the most ingenious of all printmakers however, is Picasso, who, having served his apprenticeship in sugar aquatint in 1936 on the illustrations to Buffon's *Histoire Naturelle* took up the medium again for the sixty-six exquisite tiny illustrations to *La Célestine*. They were among the 347 intaglio prints he completed during an amazing seven-month burst of energy in 1968.

One of the first attributed stories in Spanish literature, this tragi-comedy tells of a doomed love affair between Melibea and Calixto masterminded by a duenna turned procuress. With piquant humour and astonishing draughtsmanship, Picasso teased and tickled many of the images into shape against a voluntary handicap of grease. Somebody must have told him not to get grease on his etching plate: for Picasso, rules were made to be broken.

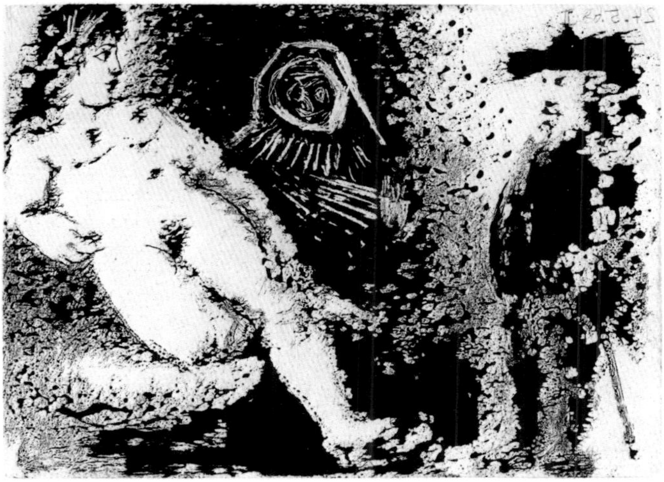

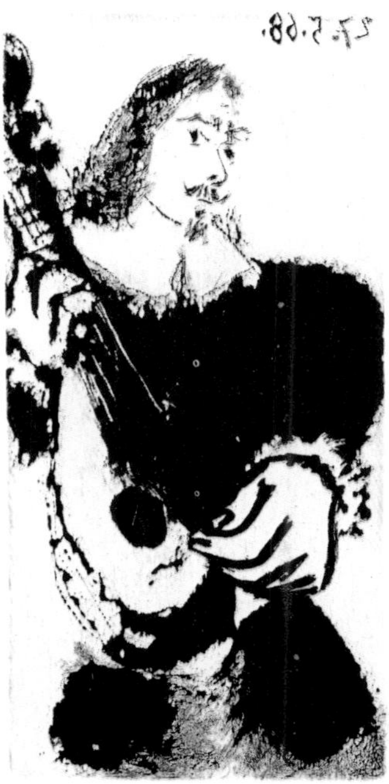

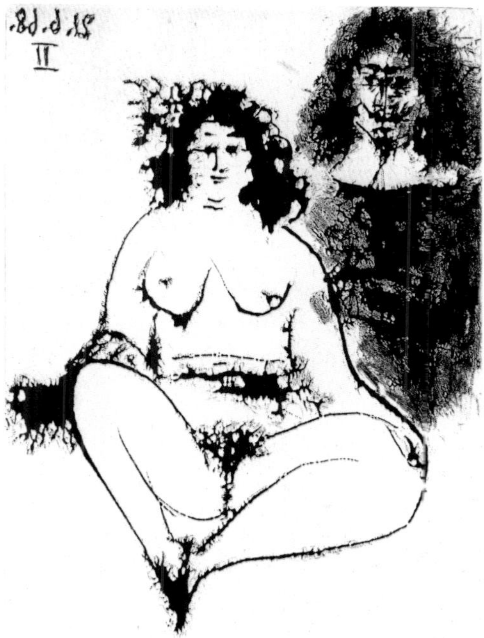

Pablo Picasso (1881–1973)

Illustrations for *La Célestine* by Fernando de Rojas, 1968
etching, lift-ground and aquatint
paper size $8\frac{1}{4}'' \times 6\frac{1}{2}''$/20.9 × 16.5 cm
book edition 66, print edition 50
published by Editions de l'Atelier, Crommelynck

△ no. 1588 24 May 1968 II
image size $3\frac{1}{2}'' \times 4\frac{7}{8}''$/9.0 × 12.5 cm

◁ no. 1599 27 May 1968
image size $4\frac{3}{4}'' \times 2\frac{3}{8}''$/12.0 × 6.0 cm

▷ no. 1655 21 June 1968 II
image size $4\frac{7}{8}'' \times 3\frac{1}{2}''$/12.5 × 9.0 cm

photo-etching

It is not true that photo-process renders an image entirely mechanically, although even if it did, this might not automatically imply abuse. In an artist's print, what is at stake is whether the method used creatively engenders an otherwise unrealisable image or whether, as so often happens with photomechanical reproductions, it distorts and degrades an original while pretending to represent it.

Michael Kidner is one of a group of British artists working in a Constructive context who generate work by systematic procedures. As Stephen Bann recently wrote of the group: 'In drawing attention to the course of investigation which has generated the work, the Constructive artist reacts strongly against the tendency to view art fetishistically . . . Quite the contrary, he suggests an affiliation not with magic but with science: with the patient process of hypothesis and experiment whereby the scientist tests and formulates his intuition of the physical world.'

This photo-etching records an ingenious device the artist made in which a square containing two circles drawn on elastic stretch fabric could, by means of bars attached to the fabric's edges, be progressively distorted to generate shapes for drawings and paintings. 'It seemed necessary,' said the artist 'by way of explanation to connect the images to the process that generated them and the photo-etching did this in a way that drawing could not.'

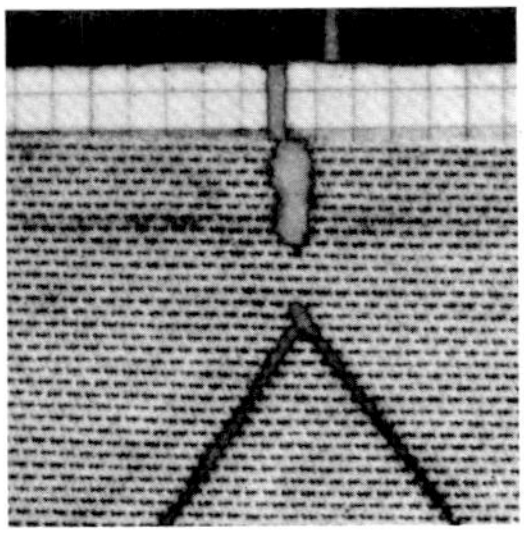

At Bath Academy of Art where he teaches, one of Michael Kidner's colleagues is Jack Shirreff, an experienced etcher fascinated by the subtle differences between one photo-mechanical medium and another. He has printed Fox Talbot's photogravures as well as experimenting with all kinds of half-tone variations of his own. He transferred a positive transparency made from the object itself to a light sensitive emulsion on the etching plate by way of a 133-line screen. Such images can be sensitively manipulated both during exposure and after transfer to the plate. The result is a very beautiful print in which the textures of wood, graph paper and the elastic bearing the astringent drawing are contrasted with infinite subtlety, winning the unanimous acclaim of the judges at the 1978 Norwegian Print Biennale.

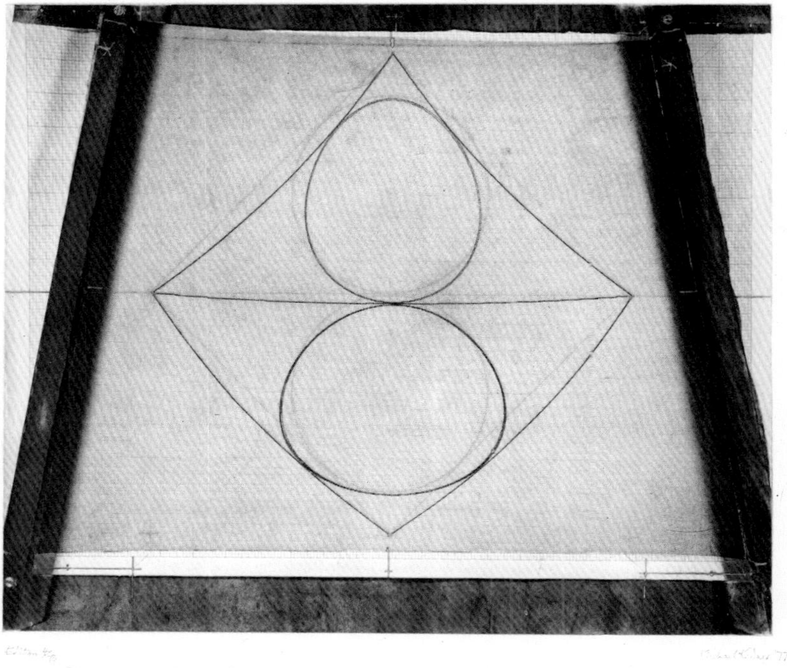

Michael Kidner (b.1917)

Square and Circle 2 1977
photo etching
$22\frac{3}{4}'' \times 30\frac{3}{4}''$/57.8 × 78.1 cm
image size $18\frac{3}{4}'' \times 22\frac{7}{8}''$/47.6 × 58.1 cm
edition 75
published by the artist

relief and intaglio combined

As already indicated, the twentieth century has seen a blurring of the formerly traditional categories of relief and intaglio to the point where certain works are difficult to compartmentalize. At the same time, prints have become autonomous, copying nothing and communicating ideas incommunicable in any other way.

Birth of Art by Tom Phillips is a case in point. It involved the systematic etching away of zinc letter stencils spelling the word ART, until only fragile slivers of metal remained. The artist's intention was to display the sheets printed at each stage in reverse order so that ART would appear to be created from chaos, as when a film of something being destroyed is run backwards so that it seems to reassemble.

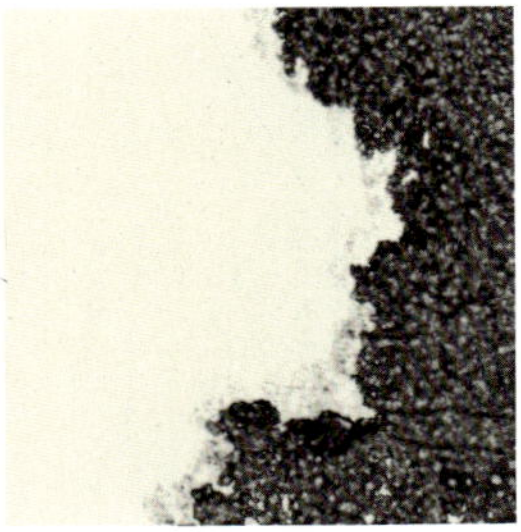

To erode metal in acid is of course a classic intaglio method, but in this case no ground or varnish protected any part of the metal which was submitted to 'open bite'. The stencil letters were immersed in acid on ten occasions, totalling sixty minutes in all, between one Monday and the following Thursday in May 1972. Each time the stencils were removed from the acid they were printed and because the work needed a small team, the artist enlisted the help of students and staff at Croydon College of Art.

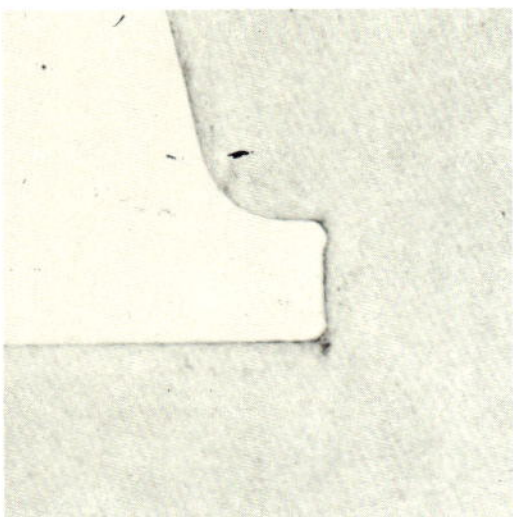

Technically it is difficult to say whether the prints are relief or intaglio. They were printed from the inked relief surface of the metal remaining at each stage but under a pressure typical of intaglio printing. This caused embossments in the damp paper to bubble up through the cut out letter forms under pressure. Of the indivisibility of idea and means however, there is no doubt. Read in the order printed, in which the figurative ART dissolves into an unintelligible abstraction, it is also a neat metaphor for the history of twentieth century art.

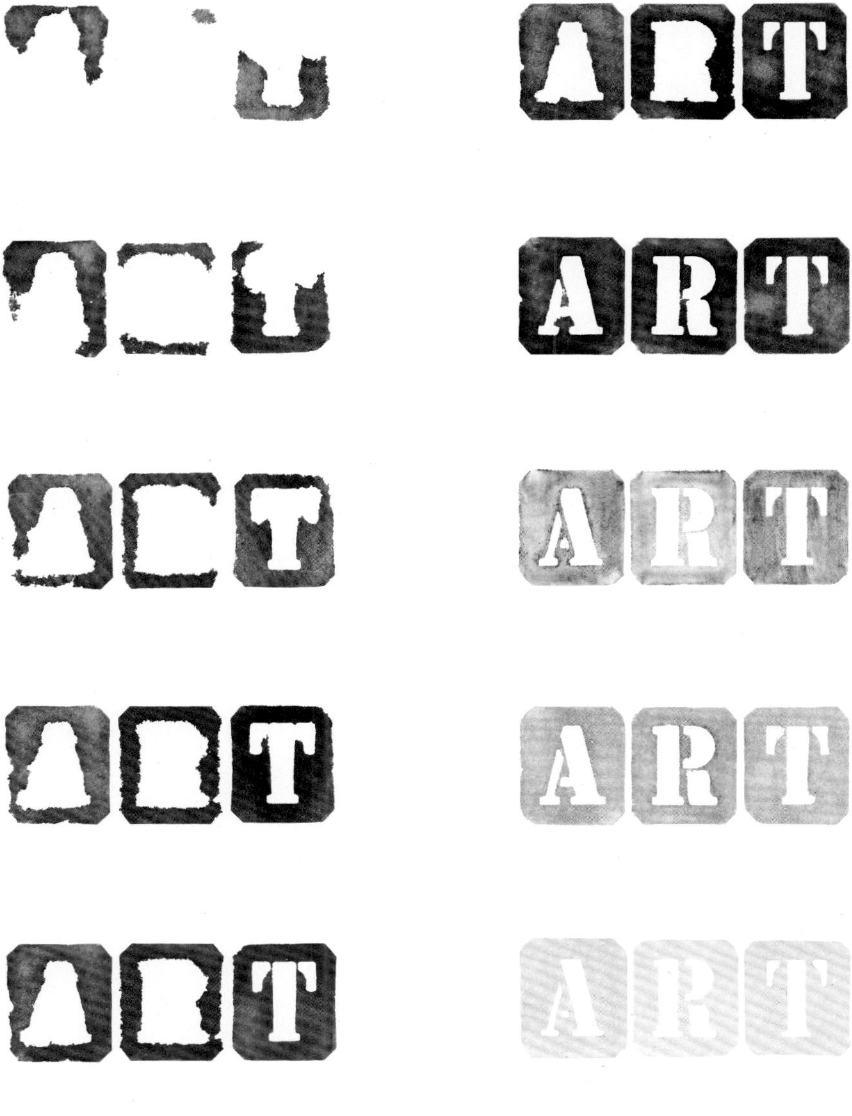

Tom Phillips (b.1937)

Birth of Art 1972/3
zinc stencils systematically eroded and printed from the relief surface
each of ten sheets $10\frac{3}{8}'' \times 23''$/$26.4 \times 58.4$ cm
edition $5 + 2$ artist's proofs
published by Tetrad Press

lithography

Lithography is generally referred to as a 'planographic' process because the print is made from an image set down on a level surface rather than from incisions or protruberances. The process, not yet two hundred years old, was invented by Senefelder in 1798. The artist's work consists of applying a greasy medium in crayon or liquid form, to a granular surface – once Bavarian limestone, now more frequently a specially grained alloy plate. When the drawn surface has been chemically treated to prevent the grease spreading, the stone or plate is dampened. This makes the surface reject ink except for the greasy image which carries it in turn to a sheet of paper. The process sounds rather hit or miss, but in fact lithography can record the slightest gestural nuances with great fidelity, making a range of tone, from a glistening black to the tenderest grey, possible from one printing. Indeed, the stone is so sensitive to grease that early lithographers, who worked very finely, were warned of the hazards of fingerprints or even a fall of dandruff! More recently, Picasso drew his children entirely with fingerprints, and Jasper Johns made a print from the natural grease impression of his face and hands. The fine veils of colour possible in lithography make it a natural medium for the painter and exponents of European Tachism found it a particularly appropriate vehicle.

In some ways lithography is one of the easiest of print techniques for artists because it comes so close to painting or drawing and is not so dramatic as cutting an image in wood or metal. On the other hand, a colour print requires an analytical series of separations, because one plate or stone is generally required for each shade. As in other techniques, direct work on the printing tool must be reversed, although it is possible to sidestep this by using a special paper from which drawn, painted, rubbed or printed images can be transferred to the printing 'tool' without significant loss in quality.

Nineteenth century lithographers (and Goya, Delacroix and Odilon Redon span the century) used many technical tricks. Soft crayons were rubbed with chamois or the greasy image could be scratched into with razor blades, needles or sandpaper. Toulouse Lautrec created a shower of tone by spattering liquid grease from a toothbrush. One can also take an impression of a found object, much as one would a brass rubbing, and transfer this to the printing surface which in turn imparts it to the paper. Max Ernst and

Dubuffet have been among the twentieth century artists to capitalise on this possibility.

Because there was no longer the same need for middlemen to translate artists' designs into dots and linear codes, lithography increased the likelihood of finding 'original' prints in the workaday world of the illustration, the cartoon and the poster. Daumier's satires and lampoons in the popular papers made the widespread circulation of the most subtle aesthetic images possible, while posters by artists such as Bonnard and Lautrec exhibited the finest art on street hoardings. There is no technical reason why posters and book illustrations should not still be 'original' prints; indeed, Barnett Freedman was among British artists working between the wars, who believed profoundly that they ought to be. However, snobbish desires to demarcate particular kinds of art as a luxury, plus union restrictions which allow only those who have served a recognised apprenticeship to work on the printing shop floor, have killed this potential.

Commercial lithography developed throughout the nineteenth century; three-colour half-tone photolithography was achieved by the 1880s and offset lithography by 1900. The latter transfers the image from a curved metal plate to a rubber blanket, the rotary principle thus introduced both speeding up production and making it possible for a drawn image to be set down on the plate the right way round rather than reversed as in direct work on stone. During the 'originality' discussions, offset was one of the processes outlawed as a fine art medium, direct printing being insisted upon for fine artists. In fact when old-fashioned lithography was revived in the USA in the late 1950s it was referred to as 'bringing back the stone age'; as Robert Rauschenberg put it, the second half of the twentieth century seemed 'no time to start writing on rocks'. It was the printer Ken Tyler, setting up entirely new standards of experimentation, research and documentation, who argued that craftsmen and workshops steeped in archaic tradition would die and only those who adopted technology and developed a new hybrid craft would survive.

crayon lithograph

Crayon lithographic medium on stone or plate produces a print which might easily be taken for a drawing itself, such is the immediacy and quality of the mark.

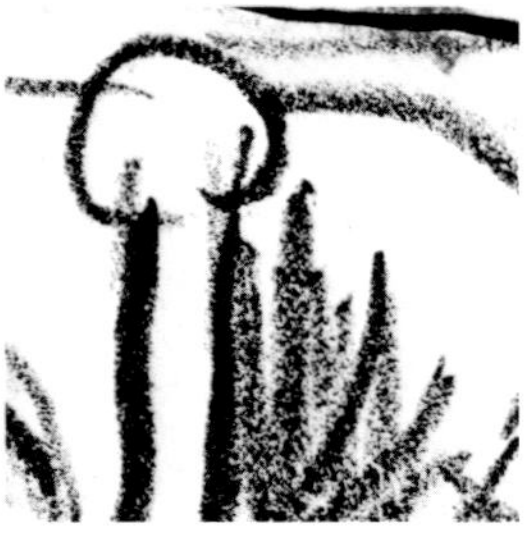

The illustrated lithograph, of crayon work printed in pink and black together with a minimum of background wash, is one of three sheets of studies made by Graham Sutherland for a portfolio containing twenty-five prints on the theme of 'The Bestiary'.

Sutherland, who began his career as a graphic artist, had considerable success between the wars as an etcher and engraver of rural idylls influenced by Samuel Palmer. Then the financial crash in America caused the etching market to collapse and he was forced to find a new direction in painting. It was in looking at Welsh landscape that he discovered 'I could express what I felt only by paraphrasing what I saw.'

Lithography is probably the medium most immediately sympathetic to the painter and Sutherland's introduction to it came after he had met Oliver Simon of the Curwen Press in the mid-1930s. At around the same time, the artist became associated with the British Surrealist movement, an association which increased his tendency to imagine forms in nature metamorphosing as he looked at them. Writing about the forms he had painted in the 1950s, the artist said: 'People ask, what do they mean? They do not, of course, mean anything. The forms are based on the principles of organic growth with which I have always been preoccupied. To me they are monuments and presences.'

H R Fischer of Marlborough Fine Art suggested to the artist in 1965 that he should illustrate a book. Instead Sutherland proposed the portfolio of lithographs which includes animals, birds and insects as well as correspondences between them and objets trouvés – dried roots, pebbles and so on. It is a sustained investigation of the irrational aspects of man's encounter with nature.

The lithographic work on stones, zinc plates and transfer paper took over a year at the famous Parisian lithographic studio of Mourlot.

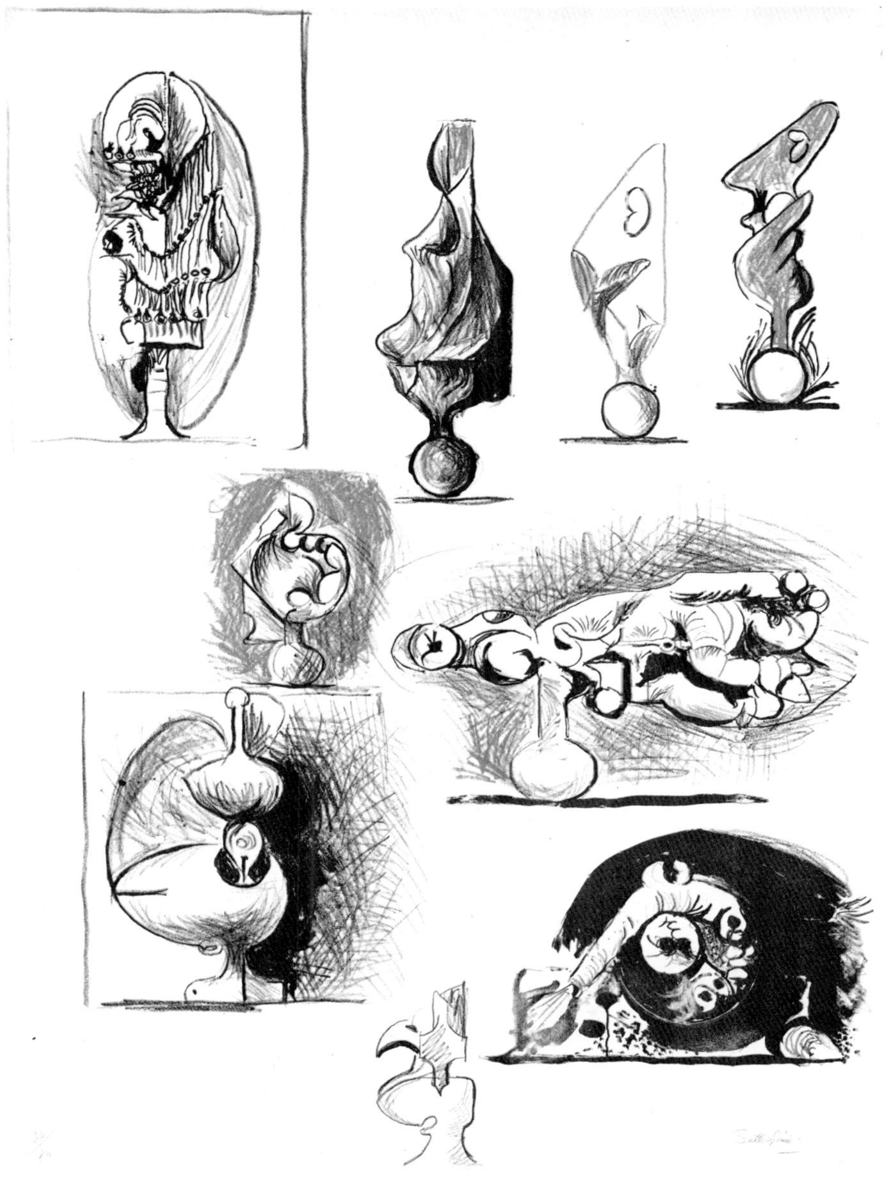

Graham Sutherland (b.1903)

Sheet of Studies: Organic Forms
from *A Bestiary – and some correspondences* 1967/8
lithograph
26″ × 20″/66 × 50.8 cm
edition 70 + 10 artist's proofs
published by Marlborough Fine Art

wash lithograph

Allen Jones uses Hollywood pin-ups and other source material from glossy girlie magazines. He says he is interested in popular illustrations of the female figure existing outside official art circles, and hopes to revitalise figuration in fine art as well as conveying the understanding that painters are making signs for things rather than substitutes for them.

The title *Black Feat*, says Jones, has links with magicians and conjuring and is a play on the notion of creativity. 'I go to some strange location away from where I live specifically to make a folio. This helps me to concentrate on the print. The notion of performing becomes very strong, because one is "on the road".'

This particular image was made in Chicago at the Landfall Press. It was at the end of a series developing out of a painting called *Magician* which consisted of two boxes, one above the other. The picture plane was at the front of these two perspectivally shown compartments and the artist's 'trick' consisted in making male and female elements appear in the respective boxes.

By the eighth print, he felt at ease with the image and abandoning colour he concentrated on the technical possibilities within the medium and 'the beautiful wash effects of lithography'.

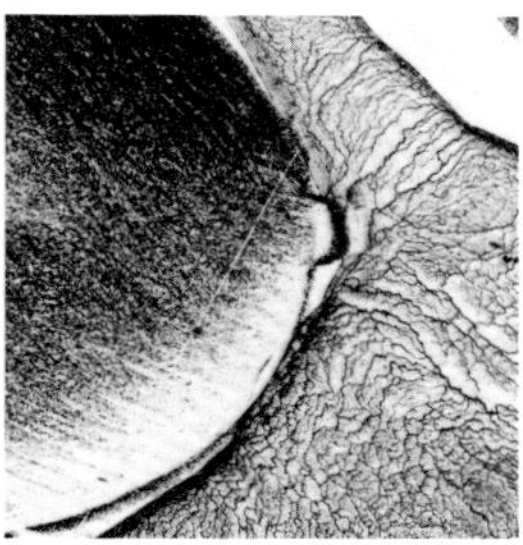

The French call such washes *lavis* and they are obtained by diluting liquid litho medium with anything from distilled water to benzine. The eddies as they recede leave a kind of contour map of their drying. Such procedures have fascinated artists like Paul Wunderlich who mordantly use them to suggest the crepe of ageing skin. Here Jones has used the wash as a background to offset delicate chalk work modelling the legs and bust and the bravado sweeps of liquid medium which have been smudged across the form. A display of virtuosity, this rich orchestration of blacks is printed on a beautiful pinkish cream paper.

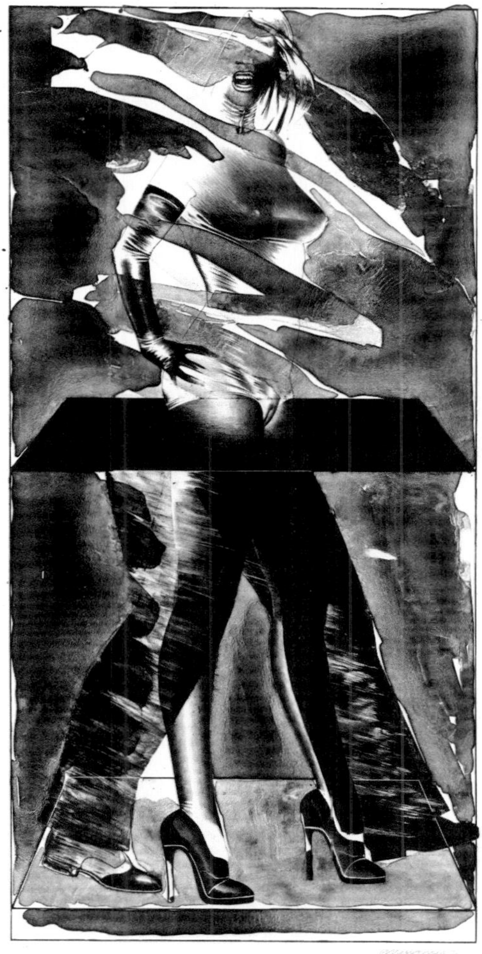

Allen Jones (b.1937)

Black Feat 1976
lithograph on hand-made paper
$41\frac{1}{2}'' \times 29\frac{3}{4}''$/105.4 × 75.6 cm
edition 60 + 15 artist's proofs
published by Waddington Graphics

photo-lithograph

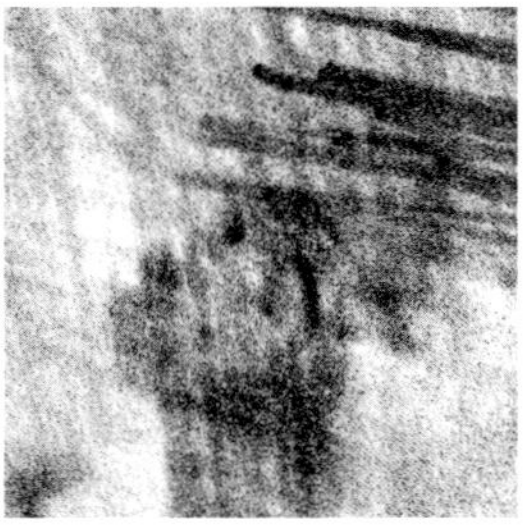

This is one of a series of thirty-three remarkable images that Rauschenberg made to commemorate the first moon landing by the Americans in 1969. He was invited by NASA to observe the rocket taking off. The suite subsequently took over a year to make at Ken Tyler's west coast Gemini workshop, dedicated to the idea that sophisticated technology and art are not incompatible.

Photographic images can be incorporated into a lithograph in any number of ways. From 1962 to 1966 Rauschenberg employed prints from half-tone blocks and papier-maché flongs – disused images found in the morgues of newspapers. He also used a technique first seen in his *Dante* drawings, transferring face down on the litho plate by frottage, magazine cuttings soaked in an ink solvent. This gives the intriguing semblance of a hand-drawn photograph and reminds one of automatic procedures employed by early Surrealists. Finally, one can photo-sensitise lithographic plates, as in commercial printing, and transfer an image through a half-tone screen to the plate by light.

Many kinds of photographic image appear in the *Stoned Moon* series linked on the plate by the artist's gestural passages. These procedures, man using technology, are echoed in the prints, particularly by the juxtapositioning of images of rocket with bird, a turkey buzzard having nested at the launching site. The inclusion of readymade photos is a printerly equivalent for Rauschenberg's incorporation of objects like stuffed goats and quilts into his combine paintings to hint at the extraordinary randomness of life.

Two of the lithographs in the series – *Sky Garden* and *Waves* – were, at 89 inches high, much vaunted as the largest hand-pulled lithographs ever made, as if great prints had of necessity to be large scale, a thesis Tyler nevertheless subscribes to. The illustrated print, despite being one of the smallest in the series however, neatly encapsulates a truism relating both to the moonshot and the printing operation. Rauschenberg described his experiences at Gemini as a 'cooperative creative yielding' and welcomed the way the collaborative enterprise made possible things an artist couldn't achieve alone. Similarly in *Sky Rite* an excited spectator of the blast-off is seen against hard-working ground technicians: you don't get to the moon alone either.

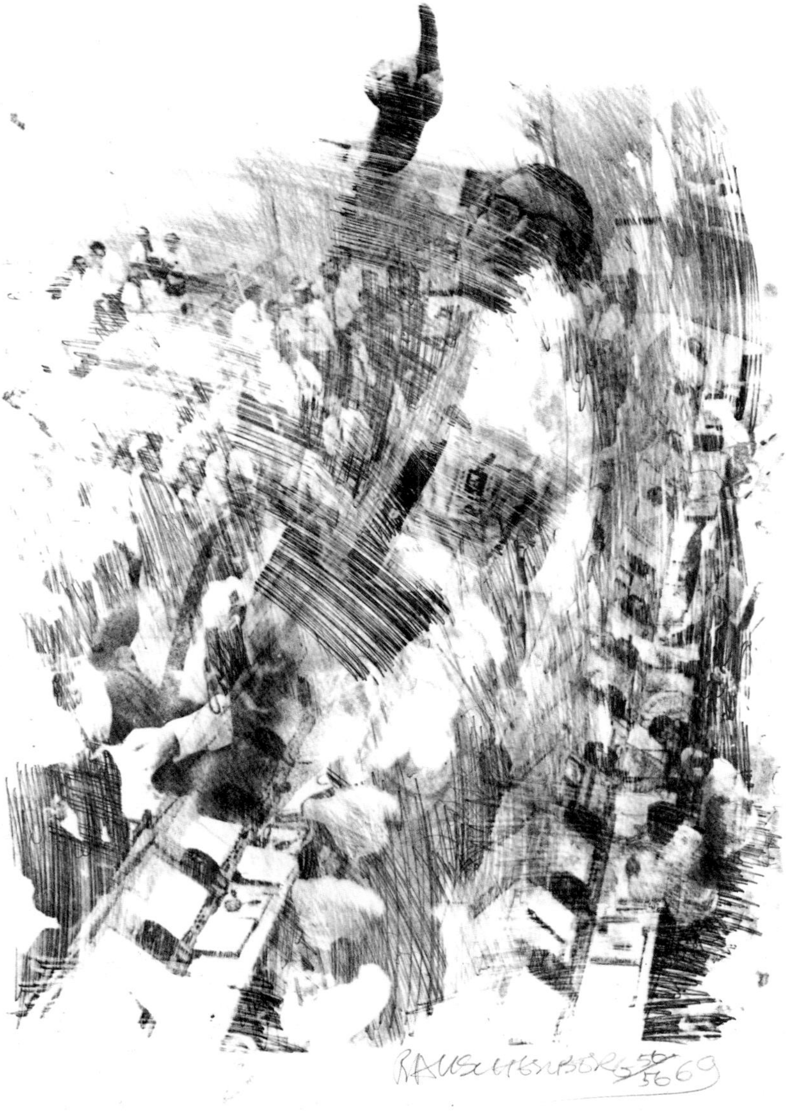

Robert Rauschenberg (b.1925)

Sky Rite from *Stoned Moon* 1969/70
lithograph and photolithograph on Arches Cover Paper
33″ × 23″/83.8 × 58.4 cm
edition 56 + 6 artist's proofs
published by Gemini GEL, Los Angeles

collotype

This process bears some resemblance to photolithography, as a collotype is also made from a flat surface. However, the image does not need breaking down into dots but is transferred photographically to a glass or zinc plate where the continuous tone is interpreted not through a half-tone screen, but by subtle irregular reticulations in the coating of light-sensitive gelatine. A similar result, also superior to the mechanical regularity of a screen in interpreting continuous tone, can now also be achieved in diazo lithography. Basically reproductive processes, collotype and diazo lithography can nevertheless be creatively used by artists, who usually draw on or otherwise manipulate the transparency separations used to transfer the image to the plate.

Richard Hamilton, perhaps more than any other twentieth century artist, has shifted his interest from nature to culture and taken a cool analytical look at photo-process as used both commercially and industrially. Sampling each of the world's most celebrated printers has been something of a fetish with him. He has also introduced creative photography into the domain of painting, concerned to show that machines are extensions of man, in art as elsewhere, and that a synthesis of hand and machine 'is not a threat to the human condition so much as a means of achieving a renewed integration of life and art'.

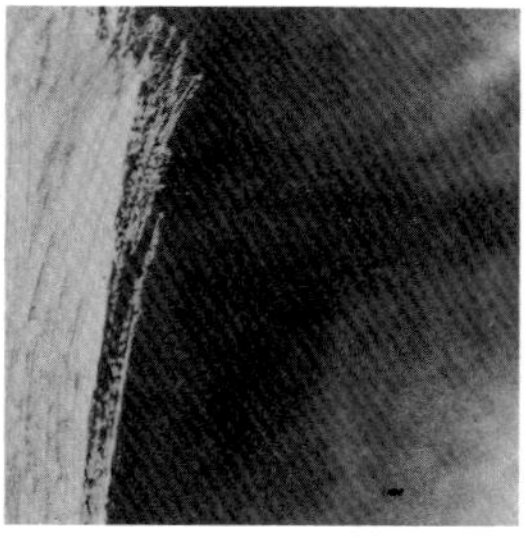

One of his projects consisted in getting several artist friends to take his picture with a Polaroid camera. Despite the alleged mechanical nature of photos, the images were uncannily recognisable as the work of their respective authors. None bore the mark of their creator as surely as that by Francis Bacon in which the accidental simultaneous movement by both subject and photographer produced a blurred multi-viewpoint image, incredibly like a Bacon painting. Four-colour collotype was used initially to reproduce the photographic image. After modifying seven of the proofs, Hamilton screenprinted eleven superimpositions to convey the rich impasto of the lilac background on one selected by Francis Bacon.

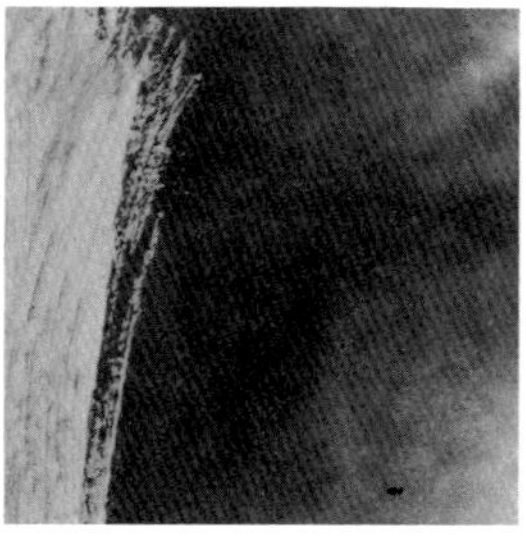

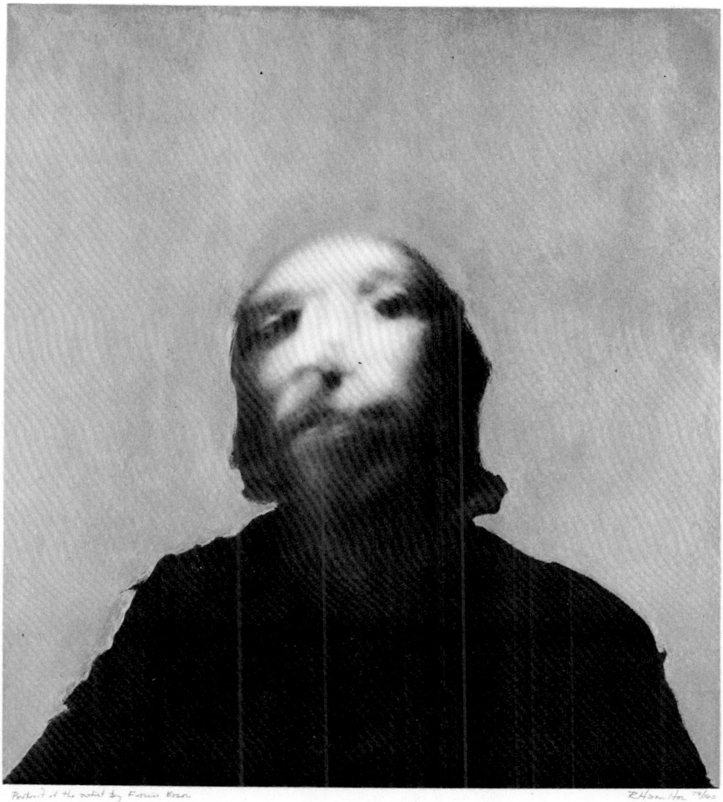

Richard Hamilton (b.1922)

Portrait of the Artist by Francis Bacon 1970/71
collotype and screenprinting on cartridge paper
$32\frac{1}{4}'' \times 27\frac{1}{8}''$/$82 \times 69$ cm
edition 140 + 15 artist's proofs
published by Petersburg Press

screenprinting

Screenprinting dates only from the beginning of the twentieth century, although it is related to the most ancient of stencilling techniques in which earth pigments blown past hands held against the walls of pre-historic caves were also based on a selective shutting out, or letting through, of colour. The history of the way in which increasingly sophisticated methods of stencilling became screen-printing has not as yet been adequately documented, but although accounts differ and the surviving material is nearly as restricted as that representing the incunabula of the woodcut, most agree that during the first decade of this century, the medium was commercially developed by signwriters.

The screen is made of a gauzy fabric – traditionally silk, hence the name silkscreen – stretched taut on a wood or metal frame. If you imagine a tray, the base of which is the fabric, hinged to a table where it may be lowered on to a piece of paper, you can visualise the simple printing equipment. The mesh acts as a support for various kinds of stencil; it is blocked where colour is not required on the sheet, but allows the passage of ink elsewhere. The ink, poured into a margin at one end of the screen, is wiped swiftly across from one end of the frame to the other with a squeegee rather like a hefty windscreen wiper. When the frame is lifted up a film of ink has been selectively deposited on the paper through the open pores of the mesh.

The technique was not associated with fine artists until the early 1930s in America. When the Federal Arts Project to support artists during the Depression was set up the medium was appropriated from display advertising. To differentiate the fine art usage of the medium from the commercial one, Carl Zigrosser, a presiding print historian, named it 'serigraphy' deriving the term from sericum (L. silk) and graphia (Gk. drawing). Although this differentiation doubtless seemed expedient at the time, to win acceptance in art circles for a lower class medium, it immediately placed an editioning process in which the 5000th print is as good as the first, back into the exclusivity bracket.

Rather than simply cutting stencil papers like signwriters, artist serigraphers were supposed to paint or crayon their design direct onto the silk, thus making it gesturally by hand.

The kind of collaborative screenprinting which developed during the 1960s however was not hand-drawn serigraphy, but a combination of hand-cut stencils and photo-process. Photo-screenprinting, which was patented as early as 1915, came into widespread use in the late 1950s. Although purists maintained only 'serigraphy' was 'original', artists quickly realised that with the help of technicians and the new processes they would be able to achieve images inaccessible to craft traditions.

Among the first artists known to have worked in this way was Willi Baumeister who lived next door to the Stuttgart printer, Domberger. In America, ironically enough, the American Serigraphic Society, totally ignored by the Abstract Expressionists who on the whole made very few prints, closed its doors just as Warhol and Rauschenberg began to use the photographic version of the medium. In England, it was Chris Prater, whose Kelpra Studio became world famous, who set the standards; twenty-five artists were introduced to the medium before 1964 when a suite of screenprints was published by the Institute of Contemporary Arts. As time passed, most major internationally known artists on both sides of the Atlantic had worked with Prater and in a quite remarkable tribute to a living printer, the Arts Council of Great Britain put on in 1970 an exhibition of artists' work that he had printed.

The medium has also been used on the Continent, for in addition to its relevance for Pop artists, it can be ideal for those working in the Constructivist tradition. Vasarely has argued that artists should create prototypes for enlargement or multiplication, rarity of meaning being more important than rarity of object. He predicted the death of 'elitist' easel painting.

As it pioneered extensive use of photography, screenprinting bore the brunt of the anathema attaching to photographic images and the reactionary backlash defending originality; it remains sensitive to economic expansion and recession through this association. It is, however, ideally suitable for editioning the images of certain artists, and since it can serve the individual printmaker with simple equipment, as well as high-fliers attracted by sophisticated technology, it is likely to remain wide-ranging in its influence.

serigraph

The American, Guy Maccoy, claims to have been the first fine artist to use screenprinting. He began in 1932 and still runs a studio which he advertises as undertaking all procedures by hand. The term serigraphy implied that instead of simply using stencils like sign-writers, fine art serigraphers would paint or crayon their design direct on the silk. They used greasy substance in liquid or stick form (often litho medium), filled the remainder of the mesh with water based glue which would recoil from the grease, and then washed out the grease with a solvent which would not disturb the glue once it had dried. The solvent opened the mesh in the areas occupied by the artist's design, allowing colour to pass through. The technique has a certain procedural affinity with sugar aquatint in intaglio process.

Although Anthony Velonis, who wrote the first screenprinting handbook, taught screenprinting to a large number of American artists engaged on the Federal Arts Project before the second world war and it was well known to commercial printers, it simply didn't enter the European fine artist's repertoire. This is despite the fact that pochoir (as stencilling is called in France) was used for Matisse's amazing book *Jazz* in 1947; screenprinting would have made it far easier to print. Francis Carr claims he was the first British fine artist to work serigraphically on pictures and began in 1949. The next notable use of it occurs in 1956 when a group of artists – among them Denis Bowen, Alan Davie and Bill Turnbull – worked at a London studio set up by John Coplans, who later became editor of the American journal, *Artforum*. Interestingly enough, Turnbull had already helped to screenprint cinema posters in Dundee during 1939.

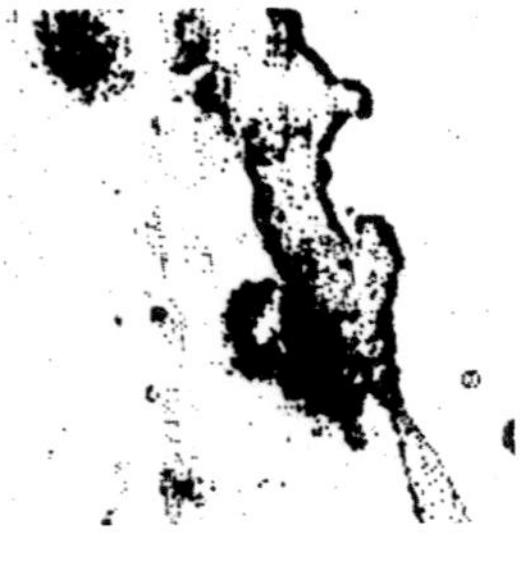

Bill Turnbull's *Headform* is a classic example of autographic serigraphy with the linen-like mark of the mesh clearly visible in the ink deposit. The artist drew the images on very fine silk with chalk and dripped litho ink; having made four or five screens, he then permutated them in different combinations, editioning four of the most successful.

Heads were among the most persistent motifs both in Turnbull's sculpture and painting between 1950 and 1957. This print takes its place amidst a volume of work in which he tried to discover how little could still suggest a head, and the head as colony, landscape, ideogram or sign.

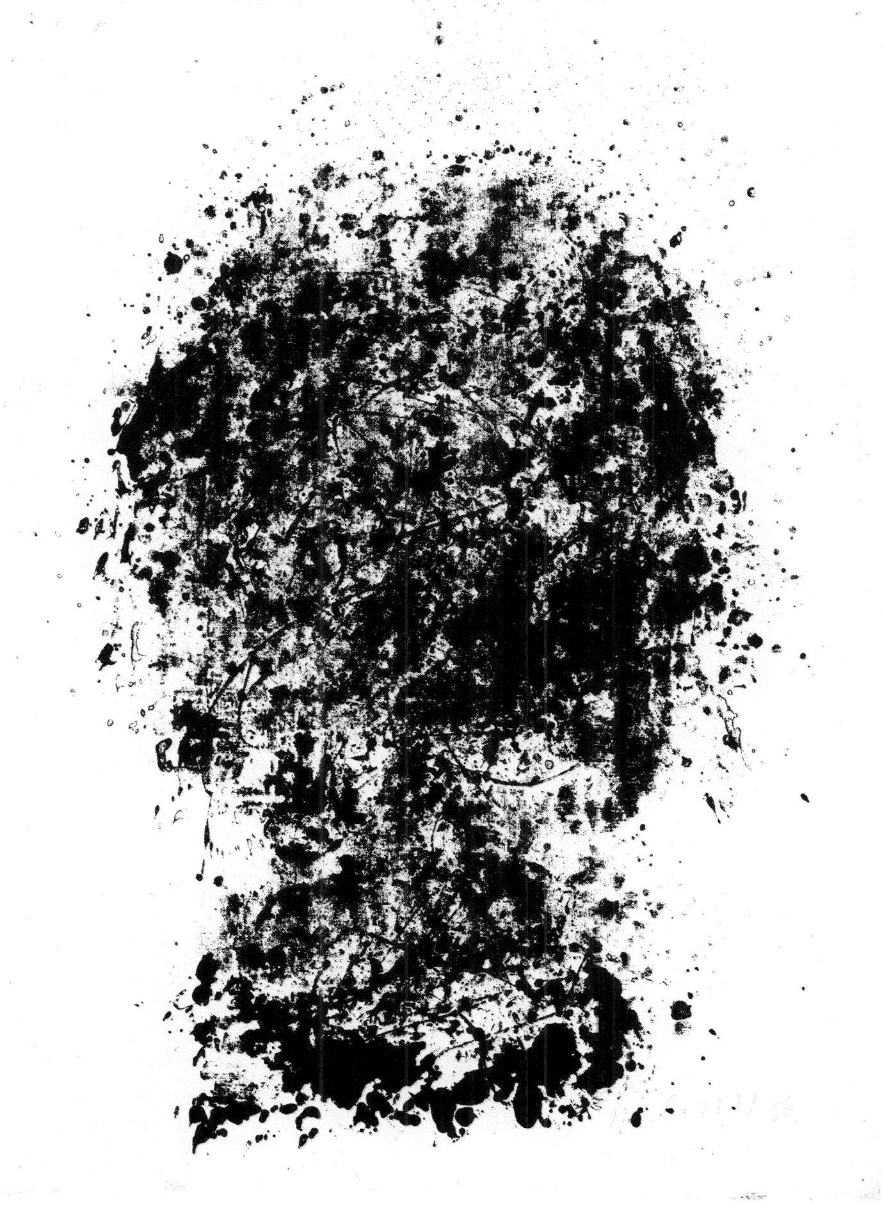

William Turnbull (b.1922)

Headform 1956
serigraph
$30\frac{1}{8}'' \times 22''$/76.5 × 55.9 cm
not editioned

screenprint

Patrick Caulfield has always made his screenprints with the collaboration of printers. He was one of the twenty-five artists commissioned by the Institute of Contemporary Arts to work with Chris Prater in 1964, since when his output has been at around half-a-dozen screenprints a year. This increased in 1973 when, in a medium hitherto little used for book illustration, he made a masterly interpretation of the bittersweet modernity of the nineteenth century poet Jules Laforgue, with twenty-two startlingly reductive images.

Caulfield's painting – on a much larger scale than the prints – courts a smoothly impersonal surface which he once said he would willingly screenprint if it were practical to make giant screens for a unique work. His imagery, with its heavy black outline, appears at first sight to be as banal as the pictures in a children's colouring book. Yet on closer inspection the distilled visual clichés prove to have been set down with an unerring eye and a satisfying and sophisticated sense of composition and placement.

His style, with its flat expanses of colour within a black outline, is ideally suited to the medium, but exact control of every aspect of the composition is so critical that the only method of preparing a print is by making a full scale drawing from which technicians then prepare cut stencils.

Because of this manner of working, when he showed his early screenprints at the Paris Biennale in 1965, the storm about the new collaborative printing relationships then developing broke around his head and the organisers insisted on his work being segregated from the 'original prints' as if it were contagious. He nevertheless won the Prix des Jeunes Artistes.

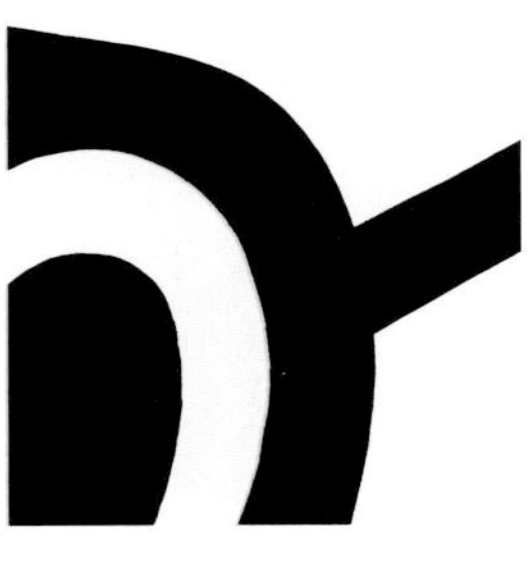

Pipe and Jug is one of a series of six beautiful black and white still lives that Caulfield made in the same year as the Laforgue illustrations. The working area is defined within the sheet of greenish-cream paper by a flat white rectangle on which the oblique line of the table, the simple form of the pipe and the jug with its heart-shaped lip are printed in black. This artful arrangement represents a form of figuration only just this side of abstraction.

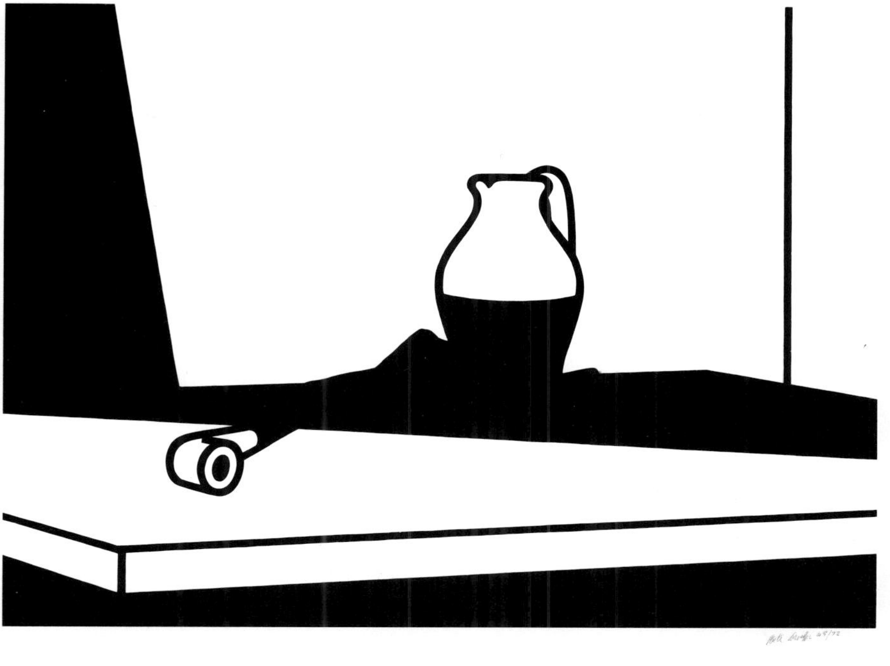

Patrick Caulfield (b. 1936)

Pipe and Jug 1973
screenprint
$28\frac{3}{4}'' \times 37\frac{3}{8}''$/$73 \times 94.9$ cm
edition 72
published by Waddington Graphics

photo-screenprint

In Joe Tilson's hands, screenprinting has become a major medium of expression. When he met Chris Prater for the first time in 1962, he discovered the two main processes the printer used were photographic and hand-cut stencils . . . 'both essentially commercial in their development as opposed to what I had seen in art schools'. So he set to work with those processes in mind, incorporating a coarse dotted half-tone screen to give his image 'the look of a printed page'. At one stage Tilson sat down and made a list of all the things one was not supposed to do in a print (such as suspending appendages from the sheet) and did them . . .

Recently his imagery has taken a new direction. He has exchanged the town for the country and the delights of technology, as expressed by the use of brash plastics in the sixties, for quieter and more reflective works on beautiful hand-made papers. For a time, however, he celebrated political heroes and Che Guevara cropped up in no fewer than four prints of 1969.

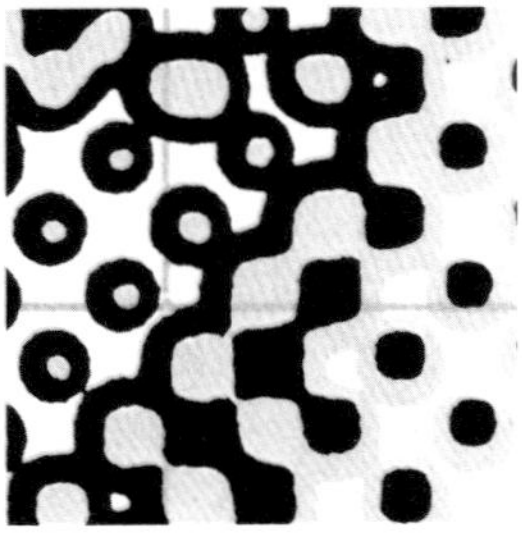

The one illustrated, in addition to beautiful renderings of Che Guevara's head, incorporated his circular name tag, a facsimile of an optimistic letter he had written to his parents, and two simulations of photographs taken after his capture and death. The photographs reminded Tilson of a whole tradition of *Pieta* paintings of the dead Christ, as well as Rembrandt's *Anatomy Lesson of Dr. Tulp*; somehow, instead of serving as a dreadful warning, they immortalised the dead man as martyr and hero instead. The image of his head, subjected to various ingenious half-tone manipulations printed in black, white and various shades of grey, was made possible by Prater's creative cameraman, Dennis Francis. As Tilson commented, the technique would probably never have been developed but for the coming together of cameraman, printer and artist.

In a tribute to Chris written at the time of the Kelpra Studio Arts Council exhibition in 1970, Tilson decided the composer/conductor/orchestra analogy for the artist/Chris Prater/studio team under-estimated Prater's role, for 'without Chris Prater none of this work would exist and be given the precise form and meaning that his love, dedication and technical mastery give it'.

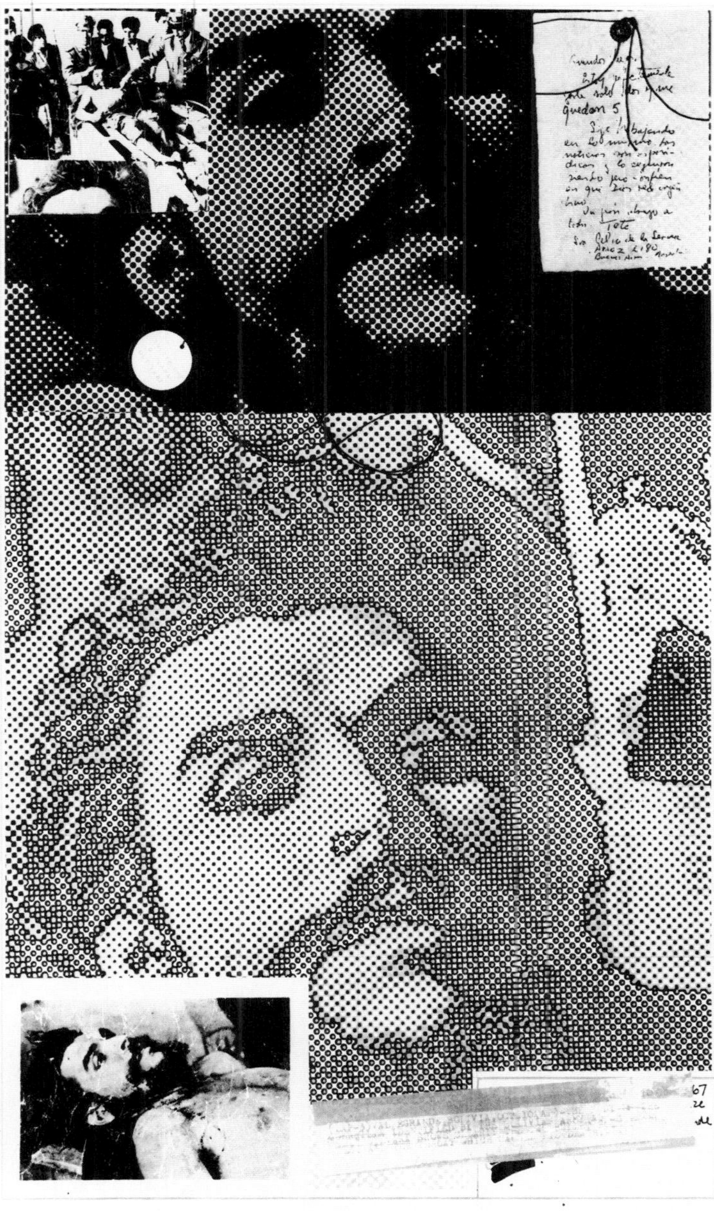

Joe Tilson (b.1928)

Letter from Che 1969
photo screenprint
$40\frac{1}{4}'' \times 26\frac{7}{8}''$/102.2 × 68.3 cm
edition 100 + 20 artist's proofs
published by Kestner Gesellschaft, Hanover

developments of the past two decades

For the most part, art, potentially one of the most creative and life-enhancing manifestations of human activity, remains an area of luxury production which emphasises the fundamental divisions in society. These divisions, between the haves and the have nots, the initiated and the uninitiated, remain almost as rigid as they ever were. Indeed, the Marxist critic, John Berger, claimed in an article reprinted in 1970 in the Arts Council's multiples exhibition catalogue *Three to Infinity* that he had yet to find an art-lover. He knew only of collectors motivated by a desire for prestige or profit. 'It is around property that we piece together our last tattered religion,' he wrote 'and our visual works of art are its ritual objects.' Among the most interesting developments of the past two decades therefore, have been those attempts to widen the influence of art which, coincidentally, have attacked the notion of uniqueness and through that, monetary value.

It may well be true – as Janet Daley argued in the same catalogue – that when selling art, Oxford Street supermarkets operate on much the same principle as Bond Street galleries, except that in one there is the tyranny of monolithic commercialism and in the other cliquish commercialism. Nevertheless, if the idea is tenable at all that art should be intimately enjoyed in the home as opposed to being publicly experienced as murals or in museums, then multiple forms of art, capable of communicating the ideas of the normally prohibitive artist less expensively to a wider audience, offer the only real opportunity for extended patronage.

Around 1970, when the average weekly working wage was £28 and a mere 1% of the population earned £5,000 plus per annum, the Economics Editor of *The Economist* expressed the view that only 'a very elite few' (one in 3–400) would be able to afford as much as £150 per annum on art. To appeal to more than an elitist minority (one in 20–30) the figure would need to be more in the region of £10–£15. Adjusted for inflation by the rise in index between 1970 and 1978 of 177%, that figure today becomes £27–£41. Even in 1970 prints by well-known artists from leading print dealers and those trading by means of special print offers in the Sunday colour supplements averaged between £40 and £80. Yet some significantly low-priced prints were also produced around that time by Dorothea Leonhart of Munich, who circulated Eduardo Paolozzi, Richard Hamilton and Hundertwasser (later known as Zehnhunderttausendwasser) in editions of 3,000, 5,000 and 10,000. Of course dealers have sometimes subverted the democratising intention behind such prints by buying quantities cheaply then raising prices to make a financial killing later when the cheap edition has sold out. The risk to the high priced section of the market is that when two works of similar quality by the same artist – one cheaply unlimited and one expensively limited – are juxtaposed, the public is handed a dangerous means of comparing their intrinsic and extrinsic qualities.

Another manifestation of the publishing boom of the sixties was the three-dimensional multiple. There have always been multiples; ancient coins, sculpture have been multiplied by casting. The idealistic aspect of the multiple of the sixties was that the art objects should be technologically manufactured from an artist's prototype in unlimited editions. This development was meant to put visual art into the same league as long-playing records and paperback books. It was significant however, that when 700 such objects, most in limited editions, were exhibited at the Whitechapel Art Gallery in 1970, only about a third were within *The Economist*'s financial limits, and many of the cheaper unlimited ones were in the traditional book, poster, or postcard form.

Printed matter – written record or photograph – has been one of the ways the conceptual artist, interested in ephemeral performance or in art as a process taking place outside the studio, has presented evidence of his activity. Technically a photograph can be editioned just like any other print form; the sixties saw this beginning to happen. Since photography has been accepted as 'art' however, the ultimate absurdity, the unique photograph with its negative cancelled, has become one of the more bizarre perversions of the market place.

Many conceptual artists, an umbrella term covering a wide range of aesthetic activity, make use of written language. So obviously does the Concrete Poet, who by typographic emphasis and without benefit of linear syntax, makes his poem into 'an object rather than a song'. Closer to literature, in print form or on the pages of a magazine, however, it is for a song that he often sells it.

photograph

One of the reasons why photography took so long to be accepted as 'art', (apart from the prestige and mystique attached to uniqueness) may be that in addition to being thought unduly mechanical, its materials have been both fugitive and unattractive, while colour is still in its infancy. Although photography ostensibly makes the most accessible images ('You press the button and let Kodak do the rest') in fact the subjective variables in choice of viewpoint, exposure and printing, make it as susceptible to significant manipulation and control as any other medium. For authorship resides at least as much in conceptual and thematic elements as in autography.

Since it has achieved aesthetic respectability however, an interesting double standard differentiates between artists who make photographs and professional photographers; the acid test is whether the idea is more important than the manner of its realisation, although cynics would say the only real difference between the two is the number of noughts on their respective prices.

Phillippa Ecobichon is a young artist, who uses photography because it is an ideal instrument with which to celebrate and serially record the subtle but transient richness of the English landscape. Sometimes she unites two or three sequential images in print form, sometimes the work becomes a monumental wall piece, such as the barleyfield she photographed weekly for an entire year. The size of an edition has often been imposed on her by institutional buyers, although she has always drawn the line at uniqueness.

The pair of colour prints illustrated form a twelfth part of a monthly project lasting two years in which she photographed Kingswell, a familiar field near her home on the south of Wight. The reciprocity in sky and shadow pattern between the paired images was entirely fortuitous; in fact the May photograph was still in the camera and forgotten when the June shot was taken.

Writing in the catalogue of a show at Southampton University where she was Fine Art Fellow for two years, she maintained that despite the absence of people in her work, she felt it was related to the human condition . . . 'there is not only change and decay, but also rebirth and renewal, and a kind of inevitability in the process from which we can draw analogies with ourselves'.

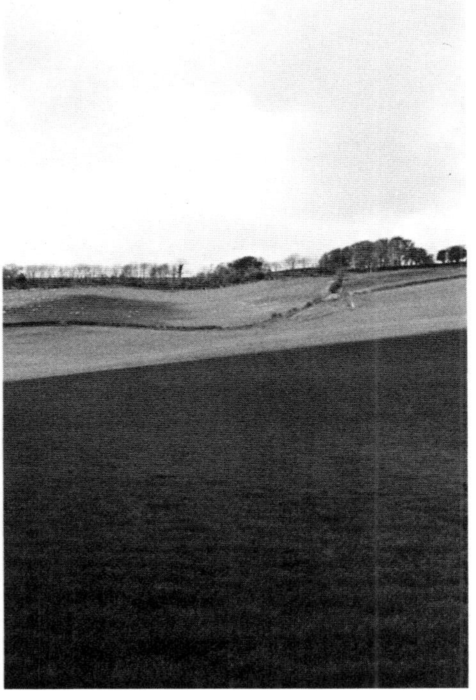

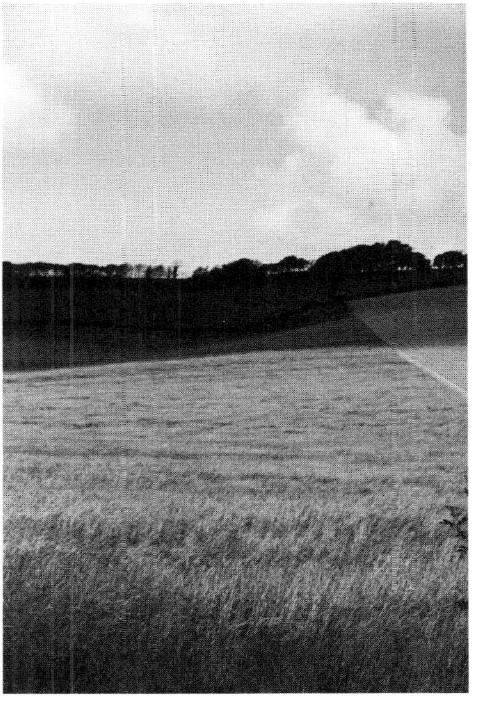

Phillippa Ecobichon (b. 1949)

Kingswell, May 15/June 15; number 5 of a series of 12 pairs of colour prints, 1977
each photograph $9\frac{1}{2}'' \times 6\frac{5}{8}''$/$24 \times 17$ cm
edition 10
published by the artist

concrete poem

In the visual arts physical form and content have traditionally been indissoluble. If autographic prints in their autonomy have a particular relevance this century, it may be that they enable this ideal unity to be repeated and therefore shared.

Much conceptual art of the last decade or so, however, has attempted to divorce an idea as far possible from its physical form; among many objectives has been that of circumventing unique materiality.

In literature, while content and basic structure may not be separated, the precise material form is rarely central to its communication. Dickens, in red leather or paperback, in roman or italic, is equally intelligible. Since printing liberated the book from being a luxury object, few are denied access to a writer through scarcity or price.

Concrete poetry forms an intriguing bridge between the visual arts and literature. A concrete poem, like a painting, may be perceived as a totality, or as Ezra Pound once defined an image '. . . that which presents an intellectual and emotional complex in an instant of time'.

Ian Hamilton Finlay, among the most assured of poets in generating such ideas, usually collaborates in their physical realisation with others; post-concrete works have appeared not on the page, but in stone, neon, even embroidery. The idea for *Star/Steer*, in which one word tacks towards the other, came to him in 1965. It appeared typographically in two books and as illustrated, where perhaps its ethical implications are paramount, in postcard form. Black on yellow, this was produced for the Brighton Festival in 1967 by Edward Wright, then in charge of graphics at Chelsea School of Art. The poem was also sand-blasted onto glass, turning it into a very different kind of object. Among the loveliest versions however, was an irreproducible screenprint. With words glimmering in silver on an absorbent matte grey ground, it cost a mere £2.

Experiencing this print in a flat overlooking the darkness of a Mediterranean bay where fishermen ply their course by means of glittering stars, one becomes doubly aware of the perfection of this particular intepretation; in all its versions however the poem has an uncanny capacity to flower continually in the brain.

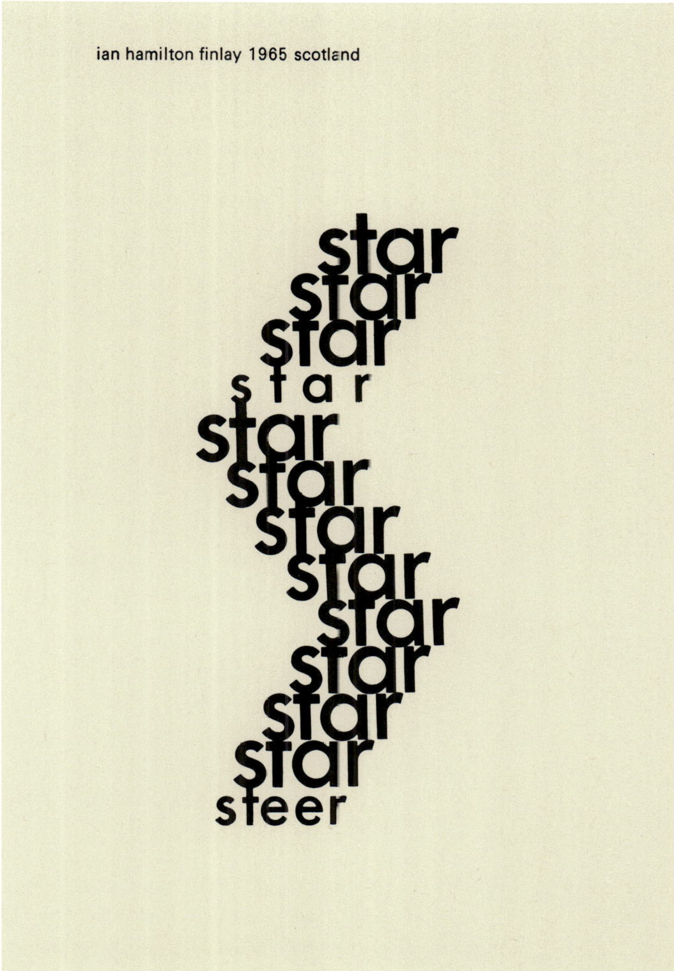

Ian Hamilton Finlay (b.1924)

Star/Steer 1965/1966
letterpress postcard and screenprint
post card 6½″ × 4½″/16.5 × 11.4 cm
print 22½″ × 17½″/57.1 × 44.4 cm
both unlimited
postcard reproduced by courtesy of Dr David Brown

unlimited edition

To be 'unlimited' is actually a physical impossibility in printing. Somewhere or another a run of prints has to stop and sometimes even cheap reproductions are in relatively short editions. What the term actually means is that one reserves the right to print more; it might be much the most sensible state for all editioned images.

In the rarified world of the limited edition however, one thousand (never mind three, five, or ten) is exceptional and comes nearer to illimitability than limitation. Long before an edition reaches a thousand, the price reduces to a figure ordinary wage-earners can afford. What rises, is the risk to the publisher, who must work harder to break even.

Since such publishing ventures must leap national boundaries to succeed, Paolozzi's screenprint, published in 3,000 copies by Dorothea Leonhart of Munich, was distributed in England by Observer Art who advertised it in the colour supplement at only £17. One of the beauties of most prints is that they require no more than a cardboard cylinder to travel from one end of the world to the other, and so can be sold by mail order.

Somebody said of Paolozzi that he matured at precisely the moment genteel middle class ideas about art most needed a knee in the groin. Accepting technology as a way of making art with the announcement that nobody expected an aerodynamicist to build his own wind tunnel, he was one of the first artists to screenprint a masterpiece – the *As is When* portfolio of 1964/5, based on the life of the philosopher, Wittgenstein.

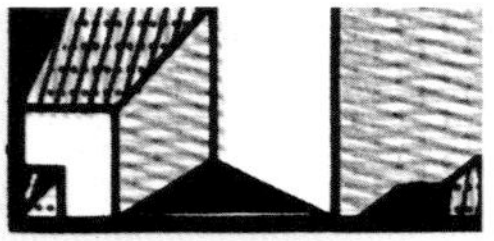

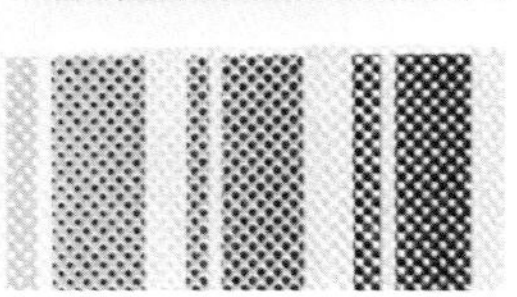

It was Paolozzi who in 1952, as harbinger of Pop Art, gave the celebrated lecture at the Institute of Contemporary Arts in which he projected images from popular culture. His early screenprints were based on collages in which Michelangelo would meet Mickey Mouse and engineering diagrams jostle patterns from Woolworth plastic tablecloths. *Bash* (standing for Baroque All Style High) is a similar collection of such ready-made images from our 'bomb culture'. From *Scientific American* to modern art, the images, scrambled together in his inimitable way, reflect the fabulous diversity which might be encountered in one evening by a dedicated TV knob twiddler.

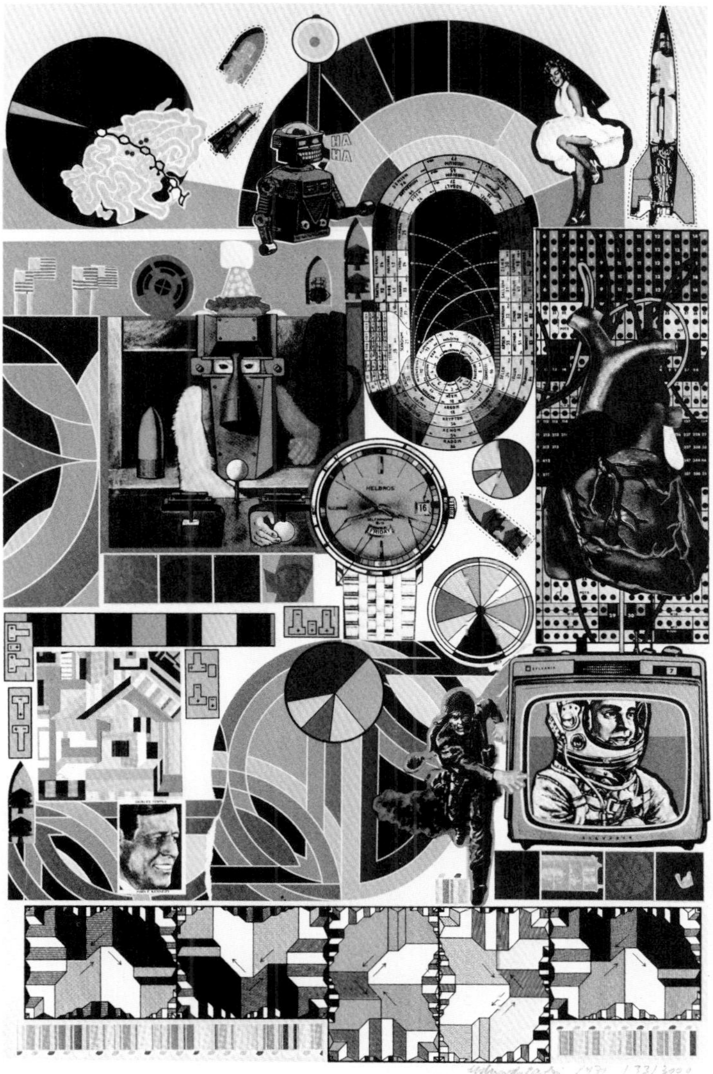

Eduardo Paolozzi (b.1924)

Bash 1971
screenprint
33¾″ × 23½″/85.7 × 59.7 cm
edition 3,000
published by Dorothea Leonhart, Munich
reproduced by courtesy of John Berry Esq.

multiple

It's hard to say whether idealism or the music of the cash register figured larger as a motivating force behind the multiples movement; both were around. As Oldenburg remarked in the script of his film *The Great Ice Cream Robbery*, multiples can be abused. 'You had people buying original art, then it got too expensive so they started to buy multiples and now multiples are up where they cost $3,000 or $4,000 for each multiple. When you multiply that (which someone showed me how to do – for a long time I didn't know how to multiply so I'd take $2,000 and they would make 100 of them and then they'd get all the money) but now I multiply and I see that if you make 75 and each one brings in $3,000 that becomes quite a lot of money. That I think is a very dangerous area, because not only aren't you reaching the people you thought you were reaching by making many of the same, but you are being identified with a manufacturer. It's very easy to make multiples because you don't really have to work them, you just have to make a model and hand it over to a technician and you can fly off to Florida or some place and live on the income.'

Editions MAT (Multiplication Art Transformables) was the idealistic brainchild of Karl Gerstner and Daniel Spoerri who felt ownership of art should not depend first and foremost on money. Trying to keep prices down to well under £100, even for works of the most illustrious artists, one of their productions was Arp's *Shapes arranged according to the law of chance*.

Arp, a Dadaist who shocked the bourgeoisie by suggesting chance could be one of the determinants in art, had a square framework manufactured capable of being used on wall or table-top. Seven of each of three basic shapes resembling his abstract sculptural 'concretions' were supplied in white felt which clings to the black felt background. Arranged by the owner they can then be held in place by the transparent covering. For the publishers, the originality of the work resided in the possibility it gave to its owner to intervene, for no 'original' had been fixed by the artist for eternity.

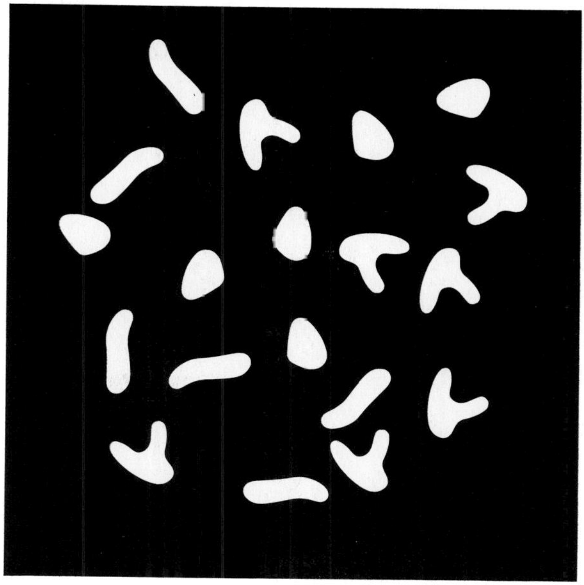

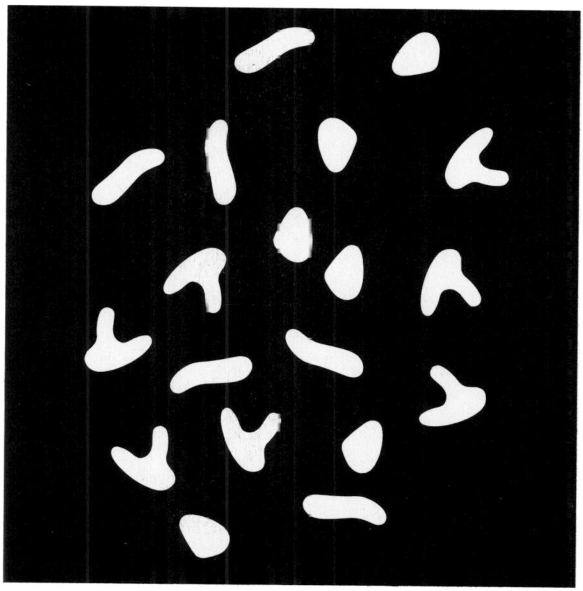

Jean Arp (1887–1966)

Shapes arranged according to the law of chance 1964
felt multiple
$15\frac{3}{4}'' \times 15\frac{3}{4}'' \times 1\frac{3}{4}''$/40 × 40 × 5 cm
edition 100
published by Editions MAT
reproduced by courtesy of Tony Reichardt Esq

factors affecting print prices

High price is often held to reflect high spiritual quality and sometimes it may: there are, however, other factors to take into consideration.

1 The fame of the artist

It is easier for the international market to elevate a few 'stars' rather than deal with the multiplicity of working artists, thus the art establishment sanctifies extreme hierarchical standards. As with Pop singers, the world divides into the commercially built names versus the great majority. That these stars sometimes make better prints than other artists may be, but isn't necessarily true. Certainly there is rarely sufficient difference in quality to explain the quite enormous divergence in price. Although the superiority of 'stars' may become a self-fulfilling prophecy (since they get more opportunities, finance and help with their practice) it is a myth that the good painter has only to cast his eyes in the direction of graphic art to make masterpieces while the specialist printmaker is inevitably a lower order of individual. Many prints by allegedly 'minor' printmakers have given me every bit as much aesthetic pleasure as those the stock and share world would approve. Any artist must serve an apprenticeship in graphic art before being able to make great prints. The market remains generally speaking, less interested in full-time printmakers because they do not generate high-priced unique paintings or sculptures. Actually society's assessment of contemporary artistic relevance is invariably built on sand. Meissonier, top-priced nineteenth century favourite is not today considered of much interest, while a pair of Baxter prints, which changed hands for £900 in 1924 when a Goya original fetched two figures, are now mere curiosities. The moral is, forget investment. Rely on your own opinion. Enjoyment is the only real return for money spent.

2 The role of the originating artist in the print's production

There are three stages in the genesis of a print, the broad divisions of which are as follows:

A The *concept*, which may be

i. fully formed in one medium without thought of a print later being made, or with the possibility of a subsequent print involving no concessions to that fact in formulating a self-contained work,

ii. worked out by the artist in direct contact with the printing 'tool',

iii. conceived by the artist, possibly in a rudimentary physical form, with the realisation of the print by printing technicians always envisaged.

B The *realisation* in which the 'tool' (or set of 'tools' in the case of colour) is prepared in order to multiply the idea
i. manually or photographically by craftsmen without the intervention of the originating artist (a reproduction, including those signed),
ii. by the originating artist personally (a traditional 'original' print),
iii. with the artist's active collaboration and control (a creative print but not an 'original' in traditional terms).

C The *production* in which the printing 'tool' is used to make an edition, the work being done
i. by technicians without the intervention of the artist,
ii. by the artist personally,
iii. by technicians controlled by the artist.

Ai + Bi + Ci constitute a reproduction; Ai + Bi + Ciii *or* Ai + Biii + Ci add up to a basically reproductive situation in which the artist may exercise control materially affecting the print in one of the stages subsequent to the conception and may or may not sign the result. Aiii + Biii + Ciii offers the possibility of creative interaction between artist and printer at all stages although a traditional 'original' print is not produced.

The area of greatest confusion for the buying public is that in which living artists allow others to make prints from fully formed originals without exercising any control other than limiting the edition and signing the results. This act can cause the price of a reproduction, which in other circumstances might be a few pounds, to rocket up into two or three figures. The real nature of such prints is often concealed by using a euphemism such as 'artists' proofs'. Because of the mystique attached to 'originality', reproductions have quite unjustifiably acquired a bad name. The problem is that although legislation, particularly in the USA, has tried to protect the consumer with laws requiring dealers to reveal the exact nature of a technician or copyist's work, these are very difficult to enact. Most responsible publishers supply comprehensive information; it only seems fair that they should in view of the effect an artist's direct involvement has on price. If dealers cannot answer a buyer's questions, perhaps they cannot evaluate the print properly either.

If 'original' prints or those involving interaction with craftsmen at all stages are believed superior, it is because where the artist/inventor is experimentally and creatively involved in the process, he or she is in a position to make demands on the technicians thus increasing that affinity between the idea and the realisation that many believe to be the hallmark of great graphic art. On the other hand, the notion that reproductions inevitably mean mediocrity while artists' original limited edition prints unfailingly mean excellence is erroneous. Even the Print Council of America admitted an original print might be 'unimaginative, undistinguished, mediocre in design and incompetent in execution and still classifiable as an original print'.

A couple of examples aptly illustrate the market at work:

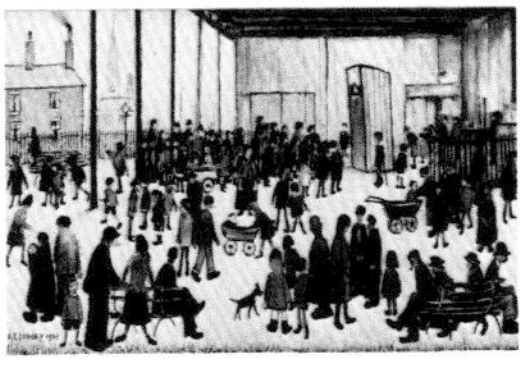

L S Lowry Punch and Judy *1947 lithograph after an oil painting*
The artist was invited by School Prints to make an original colour lithograph for children soon after the second world war. Unwilling to draw rather complex analytical separations on the plates himself, he handed over one of his paintings to be reproduced – not photomechanically, as had become widespread at that time, but by a hand copyist whose name was not revealed. On fairly cheap post-war paper (an important factor from the longevity/investment point of view) the print was made into a huge edition (6,000) and sold modestly for much the same price as a contemporary photo-mechanical reproduction – about £3. Some twenty-five years later, Observer Art, buying copies as yet unsold, paid Lowry to sign 75 in pencil and marketed them by mail order through the colour supplement. In their publicity they neglected to mention Lowry had not hand drawn the lithograph, charged £100 for the signed ones, and overnight raised the price of the remaining unsigned copies to £20. It's a common experience for the general public who have ignored something cheap, to snap it up when the price is raised, as happened here. A signature on a print is supposed at least to signify the artist's approval of the image, and was judged here to be worth £97; on the other hand, did Lowry disapprove the other 5,925 copies?

Oskar Kokoschka – unlimited collotype and limited lithograph after two floral watercolours

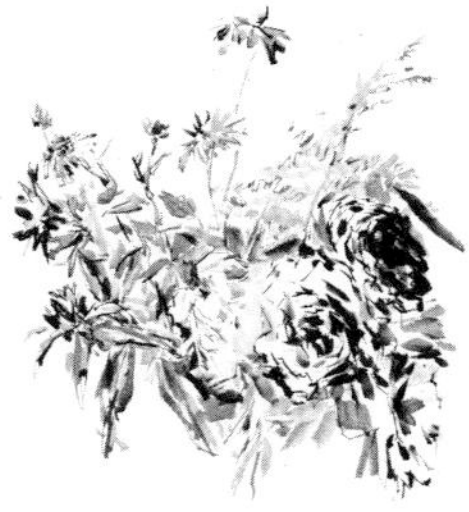

Summer Flowers with Roses

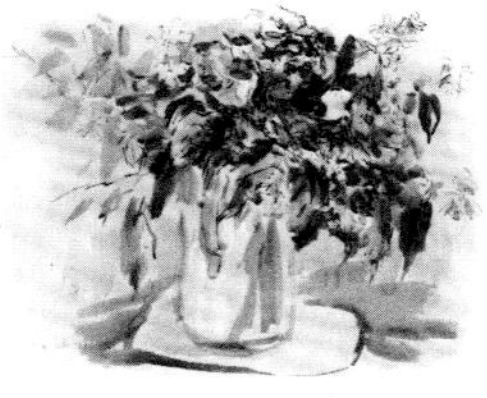

Roses at Villeneuve

Comparison of two prints after Kokoschka floral watercolours, both on the market simultaneously during 1973, is instructive. Marlborough Fine Art's *Summer Flowers with Roses* was hand copied by unnamed lithographic craftsmen at Wolfensberger in Zurich, using fifteen stones. It was described as a 'full colour lithograph'. *Roses at Villeneuve* was catalogued by Pallas as a collotype reproduction. Often a photomechanical reproduction, using a limited trichromatic printing and a half-tone screen is a travesty of an original, falsifying both colour and texture, particularly in the case of oil paintings. However collotype, which needs no half-tone, can copy a watercolour with such fidelity that the seven colour facsimile involved here could have been mistaken for the original In both cases, the artist supervised the proofing, giving particular attention to the choice of paper for the collotype print. There is little aesthetic difference between the two images. The significant differences lie in signing, limitation and price. The unsigned unlimited edition collotype (actually in an edition of 1,000) sold at £3.36. The Marlborough lithograph limited to 150 copies, each signed in pencil, cost £250. One does not need to be a mathematical genius to calculate that the return on one image will have been £3,000 and on the other £37,500 less production costs in each case.

There is absolutely no harm in paying for a signature and rarity if that is what you want, but make sure you know whether that is what you are doing.

3 The print's provenance or notoriety

If prints are sold by the most powerful dealers or seen in the most prestigious institutions the fact will often affect their cachet. Similarly if the past history of an image – called its provenance – has included a famous owner – the Delacroix aquatint owned by Degas or the Samuel Palmer etching in F H Goulding's collection for example – this may also affect its desirability. This value can only be accounted for in terms of 'aura', such as might make a loved one's gift irreplaceable even by an identical example. Presumably this 'aura' is among the factors one is paying for when one assumes that a print described as an 'original' has had rather more than the signature worked on directly by the originating artist.

Certain images become famous because they are constantly reproduced in books. This *may* imply aesthetic superiority, but it can also be a function of art historical laziness, revealing a tendency to write about what has been written about before.

4 Physical condition

There is a mystique about margins and it is financial suicide to trim a print leaving less paper than the artist intended; sometimes this is pure fetish since it is covered by a mount, but where paper size and image placement have been deeply considered, it will have aesthetic implications as well.

Another factor is the paper quality; hand-made all-rag papers, usually expensive, last longer than ones made of wood-pulp or with acidic content, which auto-destruct long term.

Most auctioneers have absolutely no idea how to handle works on paper and between the viewing time and the sale, images are often irretrievably scuffed and damaged: beware.

Look out for undeclared conservation; badly done it can dangerously undermine the paper.

5 Signature

Many prints are signed 'in the plate' which means the artist cut his monogram or initials into the wood or metal or wrote his signature on the stone; it will print back to front unless he himself reversed it. Picasso made a habit of dating each of his graphic 'tools' in this way (see pp19 and 33). The reproduction of a signed painting will also incorporate the originating artist's signature in the printed copy. However, prints of the last hundred years or so on which the artist has personally worked, normally have a pencilled autograph added to the sheet at bottom right under the printed area; just to keep you on your toes, so will signed reproductions. As the examples quoted under heading 2 suggest, appending a signature can greatly affect price. The lunacy of the situation may be judged from sales of plate 27 of Picasso's famous *Vollard Suite* made between the wars. By a fluke, about half the sheets of this suite were signed, while half remained unsigned. Although there is no difference whatever in the quality or meaning of the actual images, in 1974 a signed copy fetched $16,750 at auction while an identical unsigned copy raised only $8,300.

6 Rarity

Rarity is much prized by a market founded upon the idea of uniqueness, yet we don't value printed literature – *Hamlet* or *The Bible*, for example – any the less because thousands of copies exist. However, numbered limited editions are currently the norm. The fraction 3/10 means the sheet is third in an edition limited to ten in all; the serial numbers rarely relate to the order in which the images were printed. Because rarity is something people are encouraged to pay for, a disreputable dealer may try to conceal the true aggregate printed. A bona-fide autographic print, ostensibly in an edition of 50, could have supplementary editions in other colourways, on different paper, in different formats or even bound in books. A good catalogue raisonné about an artist's production should reveal this sort of information. Occasionally the reason for limitation is that the technique – drypoint or a tenuous wash lithograph, for example – will not survive long editioning. But most prints are capable of far longer editions than are printed. An eighteenth century woodcut by Papillon is known to have yielded 500,000 impressions. It's also true of course, that where hand printing is concerned, artists may find it boring to go on endlessly printing the same image, thus satiating the market with it, and prefer to produce several in smaller editions. More importantly, however, the art world's distribution system is deliberately geared to a large profit on the sale of rare prestige and investment items, rather than to aesthetics for a mass market. Related to this however it should be said that highly imaginative print publishing has sometimes been attempted only to meet with little success in terms of sales. Despite pockets of enlightenment, the art establishment has, on the whole, done a feeble job in education. A hierarchy, nearly always based on money value, has militated against prints and has always dominated museum thinking. Additionally, when contemporary art comes under attack, the establishment usually keeps a very low profile and few museums have taken decisive or imaginative steps to widen their narrow and elite sphere of influence.

Cancellation of the plate (removing the top surface of a lithographic stone by grinding, making obvious marks across an intaglio plate or wood block, or destroying a screen) is tied up with the promise of rarity. Plates which are supposed to have been cancelled sometimes turn up again and can be doctored so the cancellation marks do not

show. Paper can sometimes reveal the true age of a print in such a situation.
Oddly enough, rarity can also be a function of ubiquity; Japanese Ukiyo-e prints, for example, once cheap and expendable, did not survive in such large quantities as they might have done marketed in precious limited editions. Of Papillon's woodcut mentioned above, only three copies are now known! This is a salutary thought for the future; will all those thousands of treasured limited edition Picassos retain their value or glut the market?

7 Aesthetic quality

Obviously the work of some artists will prove more enduring than that of others and time and history will separate the sheep from the goats and then decide what goats cost this year. However, this is never as objective as so-called experts would have us believe and is subject to fashion as well as to chance. Did Botticelli suddenly become a 'good' artist in the nineteenth century? Thus while one may consult the opinion of experts and find it of some interest, ultimately the most authoritative opinion is that which one has personally tested, which alone is able to render a work of art intelligible.

8 Production methods

If no printer or publisher is involved in the making of a print which goes directly from artist to buyer with, at most, one intermediary dealer, then clearly a more modest price may cover materials and render those concerned an appropriate return for the work. Possibly the hope of a better future for artists not taken up by the establishment is the questioning and gradual diminution of its power to validate certain select kinds of art and totally to reject others; devolution could lead to a better market for them.

Many of the collaborative prints made by such studios as the one run by Chris Prater in England or Ken Tyler in America, however, involve highly specialised technicians and protracted experiment. Tyler for example, not only occasionally constructs special presses but has even had paper hand-made to an artist's specifications. While it would be naive to hope such prints could ever be cheap, cost would certainly be less prohibitive if shared out over larger editions. If the artists backed by publishers to use such facilities really do make the best work, surely more of us should be able to share it?

The figures below, supplied by Alan Cristea at Waddington

Graphics, London print dealer and publisher show a breakdown of the costings of a recent large 15-colour screenprint and a two-colour etching, both printed in London studios.

Note on the figures. The overhead allowance is extremely generous since it also covers lucrative dealing in prints not published by the gallery. The profit assumes all the prints will sell. Since editions sell slowly, the capital is tied up over a long period, although where a print is popular prices may be raised as the edition runs out. Inflation also favours the print publisher.

costs for each print	*screenprint*	*etching*
edition size	100	75
recommended retail price	£200	£120
average wholesale price; half sold retail, half with 50% dealer discount	£150	£90
Fee to artist	£20	£15
Printer's bill, including materials	£40.15	£10.60
Gallery overheads (£110,200 p.a. divided by 32 editions averaging 100 units per edition p.a.)	£34.43	£34.43
Total unit cost	£94.58	£60.03
Profit – expressed as a % of average wholesale price	£55.42 (37%)	£29.97 (33%)

Obviously all projections from such figures must be purely hypothetical, but certain facts form a basis for supposition. For every extra 25 screenprints in the edition, the printer would charge the publisher £42. Thus if the edition totalled 300, the unit cost per print would drop from £40.15 to £11.47; if increased to 500, it would drop to £4.23. Where a printer is employed, the artist does not have to do any more work if the edition size is increased. Even a halved fee would bring in an extra £1,000 on an edition of 300, and £2,000 on 500. Many people think we are image drunk; therefore it might not be a bad thing to raise the number of copies of high quality images, but consider the release of each new work far more seriously.

Clearly if the publisher had more units to distribute, he would have to adopt far more imaginative and active methods to sell the larger editions. However, an increased number of units means that even with high distribution expenses, overheads per print come down. The reduced cost per print *a* increases selling possibilities by lowering the price; *b* widens the artist's influence; *c* makes art accessible to a larger number of people. Publishers, first by showing faith in artists by backing them financially, then by energetically circulating their images, can play a creative role, especially by comparison with middlemen who merely take a cut on sales.

A final note on patronage versus investment

Auctioneers are always claiming record evaluations have been reached in the sale room, but £1 in 1970 equals 36p now. Thus a print bought for £50 in 1970 would have to sell for over £138 just to stand still. Few contemporary prints appreciate in the short term and where they do, the notoriety of the artist is at least as likely to affect the price as the excellence of a particular image. Any claim that a purchase constitutes an investment should be viewed with deep suspicion. Note that the price at which a dealer will buy is never the same as the one at which he will sell; he must always allow a healthy profit margin.

The most powerful part of the art establishment validates a select few among a vast range of worthwhile artists. Because their output is known and finally limited, auctioneers prefer the artists they deal in to be dead. Perhaps imaginative patronage however, means backing the living and the unknown. Whether this is the case or not, artists' prints help make patronage on a wider scale possible.

caring for prints

The best way to preserve works of art on paper is to hide them in dark acid-free boxes in an air-conditioned environment. For all light damages paper, bleaching or darkening it, or fading the artists' marks and thereby changing the relationship of figure to ground

Watercolours are specially vulnerable.

Museum curators wanting to balance preservation for posterity with availability on exhibition exist in a state of eternal compromise, although it's not much good preserving something which is never seen. Private owners without an eye to profitable resale or prospective heirs, may consider they can ignore the museum's long-term view, although most people might agree that beautiful things are worth caring for.

Here are a few tips for those who want their prints to last:

1 Always cradle a print in two hands; picking it up with one can cause creases that conservators will find extremely difficult to remove.

2 Don't hang a work on paper in bright daylight, but in the recessed areas of a room.

3 Don't hang it in a place where temperature is constantly changing – above a radiator or heat ducting, or on a damp outside wall. Paper prefers a temperature of 65° F and a relative humidity (water vapour in the air expressed as a percentage) of 30–70%.

4 Don't let your framer make you a mount of wood-pulp board – which describes the vast majority of cardboards. Make him employ the special conservation board used by museums. To be technical, the pH factor of such a card should be 7 or neutral. Acidic boards, revealed by the tell-tale orange bevel as an old mount degrades, can stain paper and, even worse, cause its molecular structure eventually to break down. The acid can migrate from sheet to sheet through time and like most chemical reactions, this is speeded up by heat and damp.

5 Don't use untried glues on prints. Never glue them down. Paper needs to breathe, expanding and contracting with the ambient conditions. Hinges of long-fibred Japanese papers and water-soluble glues (old fashioned library pastes or Polycell wallpaper type) are the best ones for securing the hinges to the sheet and the mount. Abhor

cellotape, cow gum, other synthetics and dry or heat mounting. *It's a golden rule to take no action which is irreversible.*

6 Don't use those inexpensive sandwich frames with no edging, unless you want abrasive dust to get in. Avoid contact between the image and its glazing. Old-fashioned window mounts solve the problem nicely, but some modern prints are anti-mount since aesthetics demand the whole sheet be seen. In this case an acrylic box, or a frame into which a fillet has been introduced to provide an airspace, provide the best solutions. VA perspex filters out some of the damaging ultraviolet light rays, won't splinter if dropped, and reflects changes in temperature less dramatically than glass. However perspex should not be used if there are charcoal or pastel additions to a work, because plastics exert an electrostatic charge.

7 Don't let a wooden backboard to the frame come into contact with the print as acids can migrate from that too. However, they cannot migrate through a plastic sheeting called Melinex made by ICI. Most soft plastics are dangerous to paper if in contact with it for a long time, but this one is inert and therefore safe.

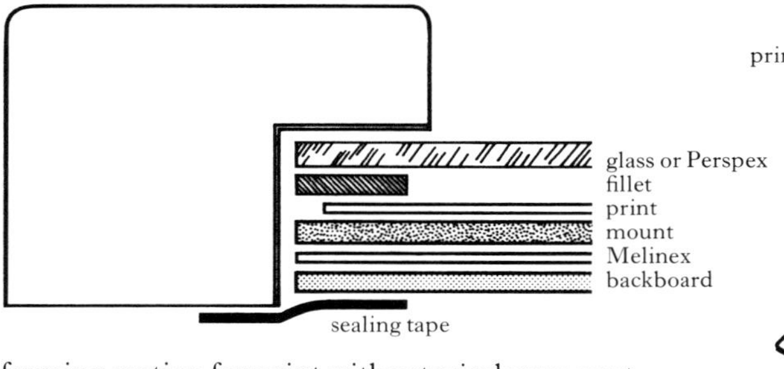

framing section for print without window mount

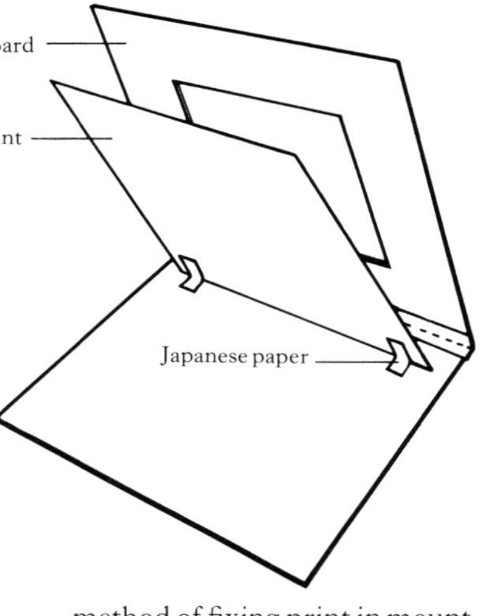

method of fixing print in mount

glossary

technical terms

artist's proof a small number of prints, taken at the same time as the original edition, for the artist's personal use. They usually number 10% of the total edition. The term has been used somewhat misleadingly to describe reproductions, especially those that a living artist will sign.

autographic made by the hand of the artist.

burin a tool used for engraving metal or end-grain wood. It has a steel shaft sharpened to a lozenge section and a half-round wooden handle.

burnisher a smooth tool for rubbing down roughness on a metal plate.

burr the furrow of metal thrown up on one or both sides of a cut in metal by the drypoint tool or the mezzotint rocker.

catalogue raisonné a listing (which also constitutes an argument about the order of their appearance) in which an historian details the works by an artist. Such catalogues become standard works of reference and should contain all known factual information – in the case of prints this would include the number printed, the kind of paper, craftsmen involved etc.

chiaroscuro (Ital. for bright/dark) referring to the treatment of light and shade in a painting.

collage from the French word *coller* – to glue. Describes the introduction of other materials into painting, drawing and prints which Picasso began in 1912 when he pasted a piece of printed oilcloth to a canvas.

collagraph an American term used to describe the printed result of a collage of a variety of materials glued together on a base and printed as a combined relief and intaglio plate. The name was coined in the 1950s.

continuous tone the gradual merging from light to dark characteristic of a photograph and resulting from relative darkening of the silver salts in the photographic paper.

deckle the irregularly shaped edging of hand-made paper.

diazo perfected during the 1960s this lithographic process employs a sensitised coating on an aluminium plate which is developed by ultra-violet light. It can imitate a continuous tone in an original without resorting to a half-tone dot.

drypoint tool a sharp tool used to engrave metal and leaving a burr which carries more ink than a normal engraved line.

edition the total number of prints made. Only in the modern period have editions been artificially limited.

emboss to cause an image to form a palpable relief in the paper.

facsimile a same size reproduction so close to an original that to the casual observer it could be taken for the real thing.

flong an impression in papier maché of metal type which can then be curved and cast as a shaped plate for rotary presses.

frottage a rubbing made by placing a sheet over a relief surface, parts of which stand proud, and taking an impression. Brass rubbings could be classed as frottage.

gouache water paint having opaque rather than transparent qualities.

graphic term used to describe both drawing and printing, but in particular used of drawings intended for reproduction by one of the graphic processes.

half-tone by photographing a continuous tone original (i.e. painting, drawing, or photo) through a screen of crossed lines, it can be broken down into a mass of dots of varying size. When printed in a single colour, these dots give the illusion of a range of tones, registering black where they are concentrated, but appearing grey where thinly distributed over the white of the paper, and so on. For colour work in half-tone, the shades of the original have to be converted by means of filters into the three primary colours and black. If a fine screen is used (175–300 lines to the inch) evidence of the process is almost subliminal; the coarser the screen (i.e. 65-line used in most newspapers) the more mechanical and obvious the process becomes.

incunabula early stage of a thing, especially books printed before 1501.

Japanese prints traditional prints made by a wood block process; the artist's drawing would be pasted to the block, a specialist would cut it and other craftsmen would print the results in water colours painted rather than rolled onto the block.

livres d'artistes refers in particular to books illustrated autographically by artists.

monotype falls half way between drawing and printing. The image may be painted onto a metal or glass base plate and then transferred to paper. The term is used to refer to any print made in one version and unable to be repeated.

niello ornamental work on metal in which incised lines are filled with black composition to reveal the design.

open bite to bite an etching is to expose it to acid. In open bite an area of metal is exposed with no protective coating or aquatint dust.

original print traditionally defined as a 'print made directly from a master image on wood, stone, metal, etc, which is executed by the artist himself' (*Oxford English Dictionary*). However since artists have used photography in printmaking 'originality' has become a good deal more difficult to define.

paper a sheet of paper is made of cellulosic fibres mixed and tangled together in pulp form in a vat. When a hand-made sheet is produced, the vatman dips a frame with a bottom of criss-crossed wires into the pulp, allows the water to drain from it as he distributes the fibres evenly in the mould, and then couches the sheet onto a felt pad. Drying, sizing, and surfacing operations follow. A monogram or other emblem can be incorporated into the wire screen and thus leaves its mark in the paper. Cheap papers made of wood-pulp (only possible during the last 100 years) are not durable. In fact they are even dangerous in contact with hand-made rag papers, because the acids can migrate discolouring and ultimately destroying other sheets. Oriental papers are particularly fine and often used in printmaking.

Pieta recurring picture of the Virgin Mary holding the dead body of Christ after he has been taken from the cross.

photogravure the commercial application of intaglio process. The image is photographically transferred onto a cellular structure in which etched hollows of regular area but varying depth dictate the amount of ink carried and printed. The hollows are filled, the surface is scraped clean of ink as the printing cylinder revolves, thus automating the process of hand-inking and wiping an intaglio plate.

photomechanical describes any process in which an image can be photographically translated into one of the print media. i.e. line block, half-tone, photolithograph, photogravure, photoscreenprinting etc.

presses although a wood block can be printed by rubbing the back of the sheet of paper with a spoon, most printing is done by means of a press. The intaglio press, which exerts great pressure, is like a domestic mangle; the lithographic press has a tympan which is lowered onto the back of the paper where a scraping action transfers the image from stone or plate to paper; a relief press usually works by lever action.

press-work a term embracing all the niceties of adjustment in paper preparation, inking and press action which ensure the best possible transfer of image to paper.

resin dust adhesive substance resistant to acid and therefore protecting a metal etching plate from its bite.

resist to repel, prevent from penetrating.

reticulation division into a network.

slip semi-fluid clay for making pattern on earthenware.

stencil thin plate of metal, oiled paper etc., from which pattern is cut out to allow passage of paint or colour.

stipple drawing by means of dots.

states prints taken before the final version is reached which allow one to follow the creative process in all its stages.

surface tone if one wipes the surface of the etching plate using chalk on one's hand, no ink colour will transfer to the paper except from the incisions. Often, however, an artist allows a thin film to remain and this imparts a pale ink tone to the paper.

trichromatic all colour can be approximated by the use of three inks – magenta (red), cyan (blue), and yellow – plus black. These are the primary colours from which all other printed colours can be mixed.

typography printing by means of type.

artists, movements, institutions, organisations

Abstract Expressionism label for the work of a community of artists centred on New York and spanning a decade from the 1940s to 1950s. First indigenous American school to win international fame.

Artists' International Association British association formed between the wars initially with left wing sympathies.

Francis Bacon (b.1910) one of England's most famous painters, but not as yet a printmaker.

Willi Baumeister (1889–1955) German artist whose personal form of abstraction suggested signs and symbols from prehistoric cave painting.

Aubrey Beardsley (1872–98) illustrator of several fin-de-siècle books, notably *Salome*, by Oscar Wilde.

Walter Benjamin (1892–1940) Marxist critic of literature and art whose essay *The Work of Art in the Age of Mechanical Reproductions*, translated in the Fontana paperback *Illuminations*, is particularly important.

Pierre Bonnard (1867–1947) painter and admirer of Gauguin's symbolism who made an important contribution to lithography and the illustrated book.

Marcel Broodthaers (1924–76) Belgian poet turned artist who also worked in France, Germany and England in a great variety of media including film.

Brücke group of German Expressionist artists formed in 1905 and initially including Kirchner, Heckel, Schmidt-Rottluff and Bleyl. There were great printmakers, particularly in woodcut and looked back to medieval sources.

Edward Gordon Craig (1872–1966) theatre designer who made a considerable contribution to white line wood engraving.

Constructivism manifested itself after the Russian Revolution with the suggestion that the artist should relate to society and use modern materials and methods of production.

Curwen Press established in the 19th century, this press achieved great fame under Harold Curwen between the wars, particularly for the enlightened use of artists for every job from printers' flowers to posters.

Concretion name given by Jean Arp to his sculptures because they were real and 'concrete' in the sense of existing in their own right and not as an imitation of something else.

Dada movement which erupted during the first world war and by 'anti-art' tactics attempted to shock society out of its complacency.

Honoré Daumier (1808–79) a great graphic artist whose lithographed caricatures and satires form a commentary and judgement on French society and morals.

Alan Davie (b.1920) one of the best known abstract and expressionist English painters.

Ecole de Paris generic term for painters gathered together in a city which for many years was the world capital of painting.

Max Ernst (1891–1976) Dadaist, Surrealist and prolific graphic artist who contributed frottage and the collage novel to printmaking between the wars.

Expressionism term used since 1910 to denote a kind of art in which feeling and emotion are paramount. Van Gogh is sometimes called the Father of Expressionism.

Federal Arts Project organised support for artists during the Depression under the Roosevelt administration.

Barnett Freedman (1901–58) painter and illustrator who asserted that lithographic illustrations should be autographic even in mass-produced books.

Thomas Gainsborough (1727–88) famous English landscape painter who was among the first to use sugar aquatint.

Paul Gauguin (1848–1903) French painter whose woodcuts revolutionised the medium at the end of the 19th century.

Eric Gill (1882–1940) sculptor, typographer and white line wood engraver who made a notable contribution to private press book illustration in England.

F H Goulding famous 19th century printer who advised Whistler and Samuel Palmer.

Francisco de Goya (1746–1828) Spanish painter and great graphic artist whose etched series the *Caprichos* and the *Disasters of War* ensure his lasting fame.

William Ivins notable American print curator and historian who wrote *Prints and Visual Communication*.

Jasper Johns (b.1930) American painter who formed a bridge between Abstract Expressionism and Pop art; makes superb painterly lithographs.

Wassily Kandinsky (1866–1944) often credited with being the first artist to make an abstract painting; one can trace his movement from figuration to abstraction in his woodcut illustrations to *Klänge*.

Sir Edwin Landseer (1802–73) popular Victorian painter who asked anything from £2,000–£3,000 for the reproduction rights of his paintings. His brother Thomas was a reproductive engraver.

Mantegna Renaissance painter from Italy who made some notable engravings himself.

Marcantonio Raimondi remarkable reproductive engraver who interpreted the works of Raphael.

John Martin (1789–1854) painter who made vast apocalyptic paintings and mezzotinted a remarkable set of illustrations to *Paradise Lost* directly on to steel plate.

Henri Matisse (1896–1954) French painter who tried most graphic techniques – etching, lithography and linocut. Much of his work was for illustrated books, including the great stencil illustrations to *Jazz*.

Mourlot Atelier famous Parisian lithographic studio where Picasso did much of his work.

Edvard Munch (1863–1944) Norwegian painter who also made a great many prints and thought them superior to his painting; he was probably right.

Paul Nash (1889–1946) English painter with Surreal affiliations who was also extremely active in graphic and applied work. Among many memorable graphic images are the lithographs recording scenes of devastation from the first world war.

Ben Nicholson (b.1894) famous British abstract artist who has worked in etching and linocut.

John Piper (b.1903) British painter and notable lithographer whose most inventive graphic contribution may have been the illustrations to *Axis* and the *Architectural Review* in which he worked the images out in terms of relief process.

Jackson Pollock (1912–56) American action painter whose drip paintings achieved considerable notoriety. Made some, but not many prints.

Pop Art manifestation simultaneously emerging in America and England in the late 1950s and early 1960s in which images from popular culture (soup cans, pin-ups, etc) were infiltrated into art.

Chris Prater founder of Kelpra Studio in London in which artists worked with screenprinting craftsmen from the early 1960s.

Man Ray (b.1890) Dadaist and photographer from America whose rayographs (photos formed by placing objects on light sensitive paper) were a contribution to 'automatic' art.

Odilon Redon (1840–1916) French Symbolist who made an outstanding contribution to lithography.

Rembrandt Harmensz van Rijn (1609–69) Dutch painter and probably the greatest etcher that ever lived.

Sir Joshua Reynolds (1723–92) British painter and first president of the Royal Academy many of whose portrait paintings were interpreted in mezzotint.

Georges Rouault (1871–1958) French painter whose contribution to graphic art included a magnificent black and white intaglio suite called *Misèrere et Guerre* and outstanding colour etchings for many books.

Aloys Senefelder (1771–1834) inventor of lithography.

Oliver Simon famous book designer and typographer who worked at the Curwen Press.

William Henry Fox Talbot (1800–77) inventor of the calotype process upon which modern photography was founded.

Tachism *tache* is French for stain or blot. The word was applied to a European manifestation of semi-abstract painting concurrent with American Abstract Expressionism.

Henri de Toulouse Lautrec (1864–1901) French painter and famous lithographer whose autographic posters covered Parisian walls at the end of the 19th century.

Ken Tyler remarkable printer and inventor who founded Gemini Los Angeles in the 1960s as a studio for artists who wanted to make prints. He has since transferred his printing and publishing business to the east coast.

Vincent van Gogh (1853–90) Dutch painter who was scarcely able to sell a painting during his lifetime, but whose work is now familiar world-wide through cheap colour reproduction.

Victor Vasarely (b.1908) Constructivist artist from Hungary who founded the Groupe de Recherche d'Art Visuel.

Andy Warhol (b.1930) American Pop artist whose paintings and prints featuring subjects such as Campbell's Soup Tins or Marilyn Monroe have achieved world-wide notoriety.

James McNeill Whistler (1834–1903) American artist who worked in Europe and achieved great renown for his minimal etchings of Venice which encouraged the phenomenal popularity of that medium until the Depression.

Carl Zigrosser eminent American print curator and historian who proselytized for screenprinting as a fine art form and wrote the extremely useful *Guide to the Collecting and Care of Original Prints*.